HOW I CAN EXPERIENCE GOD

D0107892

Books by the same author:

Answers for Youth Series:

    How Far I Can Go
    How I Can Be Real
    How I Can Experience God
    How I Can Fit In
    How I Can Make Decisions

Creative Bible Study
A New Face for the Church
69 Ways to Start a Study Group
A Theology of Christian Education
Three Churches in Renewal
Youth Ministry

ANSWERS FOR YOUTH SERIES

HOW I CAN EXPERIENCE GOD

LARRY RICHARDS

Illustrations by Charles Shaw

ZONDERVAN
PUBLISHING HOUSE

OF THE ZONDERVAN CORPORATION
GRAND RAPIDS, MICHIGAN 49506

How I Can Experience God
Copyright © 1979 by The Zondervan Corporation

First published in 1969 by Moody Press, Chicago, under the title *Is God Necessary?* Copyright © 1969 by Moody Bible Institute.

Zondervan Revised Edition   1979

Library of Congress Cataloging in Publication Data

Richards, Lawrence O
   How I can experience God.

   (Answers for youth)
   Published in 1969 under title: Is God necessary?
   Includes bibliographical references.
   SUMMARY: Discusses the reasons for believing in the existence of God and ways of making God part of one's life.
   1. God.   2. Youth—Religious life.
   [1. God.   2. Christian life]   I. Title.
   BT102.R5   1979   231   79-19799
   ISBN 0-310-38991-7

Printed in the United States of America

Contents

1

Out of focus

spend a lifetime seeking for a god who isn't there
   thinking in our hearts that nothing's fair
try so hard but seems he doesn't care
     how we feel

confused, in the shadows of decision
   crying in the dark for just a vision
of the one who can release us from the prison
     of our minds

in search of friends, a way to be free
   all they offer; a dream and LSD
fantasy, illusion, loss of reality
     bordering insanity

where is god? can't he see
   the twisted lives so doomed by hell's decree
what of Christ's blood on calvary
     33 A.D.

reach up and touch the sky
　touch the stars and wonder why
why the god who made them doesn't try
　　　to understand

this god's too small for a shook-up generation
　what kind of god do you relate to every nation
is god love, security, peace and our salvation
　　　from this mess?

Life had hit Rick hard when he wrote this poem. It was his second year in college. Suddenly all the answers he'd heard from his missionary parents, all the neat formulas from Sunday school, faded like a mist.

There were lots of things that upset his life. Having to leave a sports team he loved. Setting his heart on things

he was pretty sure he shouldn't have. But it all fell into place when he took over a Sunday school class of eleven-year-olds and tried to mouth to them the words he was told when he was in Sunday school. Words—he realized, even as he spoke them—that simply were not real to him.

Rick isn't the only person to take a look at his faith, and suddenly find that everything is so out of focus that it seems unreal.

"I used to pray and pray," says a Michigan high school girl, "and felt God was failing me. I started doing things that God would be displeased with. I felt that my life was caving in on me. Even though I prayed and read my Bible, it didn't seem to mean much to me."

There are lots of things that start a young person's faith "caving in on me." Sometimes the doubts come from subjects discussed at school. A fifteen-year-old from New Jersey says, "In history we talked about the scientific theories of how the earth evolved and that man developed from an apelike creature. I, along with many other in the class, began to question if God really existed." But usually the high schoolers and collegians who helped with this book found that doubt was keyed by their personal experience, and their failures to see evidence of God acting in their lives.

A Pennsylvania girls says, "Doubts in my life arise when I see other people who aren't Christians seemingly having more fun in life. And also as I see other people that live good lives and are really outstanding people. They seem to be having full lives without Christ. So maybe it's not necessary to have Christ after all." To a Michigan fellow this ties in with the poor example he's noticed given by Christian adults. "If there's no real evidence in the Christians that this is a better way than the non-Christian way, why should one accept it?"

"This is the biggest stumbling block to me," says a senior. "I know many church people who preach one thing and do another. I know a preacher who tears down the young people of his church for not acting like Christians. Yet one of his daughters is pregnant before she is married. I've seen this happen with laymen too. They cut down the acts of youth while their own children are living a wrong life.

"I know other Christian kids who will say lying is wrong and yet when it comes to a sticky part in their life they are willing to 'stretch a point' because it is only going to be a 'white lie.' Then—because this happens so often —people, so-called Christians, say they can't help it because they are only human. But they don't even ask the Lord's forgiveness or *try* to live a more perfect life or *try* to be like Christ."

A child might miss all the inconsistencies between what people profess and how they live. But a young person? Never. And any thinking, honest teen or twenty-year-old is going to wonder if there's any reality to a Christianity that seems to break down so tragically when put under the pressure of daily life!

But daily life is experienced, and not just observed. Sometimes guys and girls have reason to wonder where God is in their *own* lives.

"I was the most unpopular girl in school," shares a New Jersey junior. "I cried myself to sleep almost every night. I even went so far as to say there was no God. I thought, if there was a God how could this happen to me?"

As an Evanston, Illinois, sophomore says, "When something happens to hurt a teenager, he naturally has doubts. If his parents get killed in an accident, he says, 'Where was God when that happened?' Even more minor pains, such as losing a steady, can cause doubts. I don't know how such questions can be answered, but I hope somebody finds out, because I have doubts too."

"Kids are taught from the time they are real little," adds another, "that if they pray to God and Jesus, the right thing will happen. So when they grow older, they say, 'God help me.' And when God doesn't, they are disillusioned about God and Christianity."

It's true. Sometimes our experience just doesn't square with the answers we've been given. Or with the glowing tales of transformation we've heard. "Lots of kids doubt," says one senior, "because nothing very exciting ever happens in their everyday lives. Preachers talk about 'abundant life,' but we never know what it really is."

"I am thankful to Christ for redemption and salvation," writes an Ontario sixteen-year-old, "but in everyday life it all seems so remote. Through devotions I have found Christ's love fresh in the morning, but after that is over it all seems so distant again. It has been a disadvantage in a way to have always had Christian answers and doctrine thrown at me. I know far more answers with my head that with my heart. How can Christ become a reality to me? How does one get the things of Christ to be more of a thing which exists in reality?"

"I often wonder if the Bible is really true," admits a Kansas fellow. "How do we know it isn't a man-made fairy tale? But then I think that it would be difficult for a mere man to think up something so fantastic. I believe that the Bible is true, and that God is relevant today. And I read about how other people have had real experiences with God. But when I try it doesn't work. Then I wonder. Is there a God that can help us today?"

And so doubts come.

The simple solutions we were taught as children don't seem to solve anything. Prayer doesn't seem to change things we so desperately want changed. People disappoint us. And the "Christian life" as we're living it is far from the "abundance" we've been promised.

And so, like Rick, we may suddenly realize, even as we speak to them, that the words we mouth about God simply are not real to us.

What about doubt?

"Too many adults," complains a Biola College student, "have the attitude that doubts are bad and that you are not a Christian if you have doubts. They don't offer many good answers or solutions to the problem. They just criticize. Many teenagers wonder, 'Why do I doubt?' What can I do that is practical for someone my age, to have more faith and less doubts? Is doubt normal? Why do adults think I'm not saved when I wonder about what the Bible says and ask questions? Don't adults ever have doubts and wonder about things? Why does everyone look at me like I'm a dumb kid when I ask questions?"

Usually kids who've worked their way through most of their doubts have a very different viewpoint. "Honest doubts about Christianity are caused by the fact that most people today have only a shallow, hearsay view of Christianity," says a Washington nineteen-year-old. "Honest doubts are good."

And this squares with the experience of Judy, a Midwesterner who writes, "I was brought up in a Christian home, never questioning Christianity. It was my way of life. Why did I go through a period of doubting? Because I honestly realized I had nothing. I looked at people in my church. What did they have? Nothing, as far as I could see. It was all a farce. I had no purpose in life, no reason for being a Christian—my life was a mess and I was desperate. So I started at the very beginning, and had a real battle with God.

"As I look back, I am extremely thankful for this period in my life. It was actually an introduction to a vital relationship with my Lord. I would not trade it—for He taught me so much. I now have a relationship with Him that I would not have believed possible a year ago."

So a time of doubting can lead to the fabled "happy ending." Doubts can be a good thing. A time of breaking out of a secondhand, childhood type of faith into a mature faith. A real faith. At least, it seems to have for Judy.

But it doesn't always work out this way. A Florida girl says, "No, God is not in the least necessary to my life. My own religious convictions now begin and end in my relationships to people. To me, 'God' is merely a label for those things men know little of but must explain."

Others too come up with a nonbiblical faith, like the one described by this California girl. "God is necessary, in the sense that love, understanding, and communication are necessary. God is the most important part of man—perhaps that may be called 'the Force.' God is in everybody, and the content of a person's life depends on the degree to which he lets this Force, or God, show. A person cannot tell if there is a heaven or hell until he dies. Reincarnation is not impossible. A person cannot know if there is a purpose to life. No one can be sure of anything. In fact, no one can be sure if God is necessary."

Doubt, then, isn't always a doorway to the faith and the "reality" described in the Bible. It may lead elsewhere. Or nowhere. As it has for Carl, from Oregon, who says, "I just accept the fact that the odds are in favor of there being a God. I often have doubted and still do doubt that God is relevant." And eighteen-year-old Jill: "Just within the past two years I have started to question the relevancy of

God. Now I feel that although God is a great foundation, He has no part in my daily life."

So, what about doubt?

For one thing, it's normal. There comes a time in almost everyone's life when he doubts his faith—when it becomes "unreal." Usually this is a sign that we're shrugging off childhood and the unthinking acceptance of the beliefs of our parents and Sunday school teachers. It's a sign that we're ready to work out a *personal* faith that can be real and solid for us—not just for "them."

And here's an interesting thing about doubt. In a sense, doubt is an invitation. An invitation to examine a whole maze of *possibilities*: possibilities that were denied to us as long as our "faith" existed as a secondhand imitation of the faith of others. Doubt is an invitation to step out and to *find reality for ourselves*. Is God necessary? Is God *there?* Can we find Him, know Him, for ourselves?

But doubt is a threatening invitation. If we accept *possibilities*, we admit to ourselves that God may not be there. This is too much for some. They shrink back from the invitation. They bar the door to doubt, and hide behind the words and the rules of "Christian respectability." But underneath it all, they're usually afraid, wondering still if maybe it isn't real after all. (That's one reason why some adults react so violently to questions youth ask!)

Probably you've already felt doubt's compelling invitation. And probably you're ready to accept it. Ready to step outside the safety of "their" faith to find reality for yourself. What might our exploration together mean to you?

Live options

What possibilities did the teens and twenties who contributed their experiences to this book see?

To some, the "unreality" of a questioned faith was only apparent. The fault was not in what was believed, but in the believer.

"My teen years," says a Montana twenty-one-year-old, "were years when I felt I was left hanging. They seemed indecisive years of wandering in circles. I had the message of Christ and my responsibility to others, but it was a load too big to handle. How could I begin to carry it when I saw no spiritual vitality and a lot of bickering in my own church? So there I was, getting my high school education and stumbling around in my own moral mixups. I was no rabble-rouser, just an unfocused Christian. I was ashamed to take anyone to the inauspicious meetings which were held just off the school grounds once every two weeks. In fact, I skipped them unless a fellow Christian insisted once too often. It all seemed so childish. It's not that I didn't want to live for Christ. But it was no use."

Lots of kids have felt like this, and later looked back and seen that *they* were out of focus, not Christ. "I personally have doubted the relevancy of God in my life," writes a Wheaton College senior. "In my church-centered environment I never really saw the person of Christ as much as the code of conduct people gave Him credit for establishing. So in high school I concluded that Christ came to make restrictions on my life. Hardly an 'abundant life!' College meant I could begin to build my future around my own happiness. I didn't have enough guts to be cold on the idea of Christ, so I did the standard occasional-devotional bag, and proceeded to live my own life.

"In my sophomore year of college, I met some visiting guys on campus who *obviously* had some dimension to their lives I just did not have. They explained that it was a relationship with a Person, Jesus Christ, and proceeded to tell me how they quit trying to change their lives and please God, and asked Christ to change them. That was the beginning of an honestly new life for me—no more phoniness, hypocrisy, or performance. Just a day-by-day, minute-by-minute walk of dependence upon Christ. It's really out of sight!"

Maybe this is for you. Maybe as you think through this book you'll find some childhood ideas about Christianity cleared away, and get a clear focus on Christ. And maybe, just maybe, your life will also go way "out of sight" as you experience Him in a new way.

But this isn't the only option.

It's possible that the conclusion you'll come to is that you just can't believe in the God of the Bible. That He isn't real. It's an option. A possibility. And we might as well face it.

Another option suggested by many of my correspondents is that God is real, but He's completely irrelevant to our lives. "The basic fact is," one fellow suggests, "that there's a real possibility we can get along just as well without God, and cut out half the trouble!"

"God is something you can't deny," says another. "That's too bold. But God has no relevance to teens, seemingly, and no matter who or what He is, it wouldn't make any difference in our lives." "I'm doing OK," adds another. "Why should I let God take over? Besides, I see kids who say they have God, out in the cold when some fun stuff goes on. I don't want to be out of the groove, so God isn't necessary because He doesn't like fun."

And it could be that this is what you'll conclude. That God is probably "out there" somewhere, but that He isn't acting in our world, or in our lives. And so God isn't really relevant. Not now. Not daily. And not needed.

There are other options. We'll look at them as we go on. And all along the way it will be up to you. Up to you to make your own decisions, and your own choices. And your own discovery of how *you* can experience God.

Steps to take

These questions will help you take a look at yourself before you read on. Here's what to do:

1. Have you had that "unreal" feeling about your faith too? Take a moment and jot down *what* you doubt, and *why*.

2. What, to you, would be necessary to show the "reality" of a faith?

3. What does the phrase "experience God" mean to you? Do you feel that you do experience Him now? If so, how?

2

The grass is greener

"A great many people," a contemporary writer notes, "do not bother with God. They couldn't care less. And they get along without Him. At least, it seems that they do. They do not lose their jobs or get cancer. They have a good time. And God does not seem to spank them. In fact, they seem to get along every bit as well as those who do bother with God."[1]

As the girl quoted last chapter noted, "They seem to be having full lives without Christ. So maybe it's not necessary to have Christ after all."

That's right. The grass *is* greener on the other side of the fence.

That's especially easy to believe if you've been brought up in a Christian environment (with at least some of its characteristic don'ts), and have finally been hit hard by that fuzzy, out-of-focus feeling.

Wondering about God, and not having Him seem very real in your own life, it's only natural to look around at others and feel, as one guy, that God would seem a lot more necessary "if the world didn't have such a ball without His help!"

One college student who wrote me said that anyone writing a book like this one should "realize that many people live happily without God, and few live happily with Him." Well, that's pretty hard to prove either way. But it is true that millions and millions of people do go through life with scarcely a thought of God. And they talk about "happiness" as well as despair.

Yet, most of the kids who wrote in didn't picture the world quite this way. They didn't see God (as did Freud) as the one big hangup who keeps us all from being natural and happy and free. And they didn't envy people without a faith.

"For a long time," says an Illinois eighteen-year-old, "I thought I was the only one in the world with any problems, and that the non-Christians got along better than Christians. As I got to know people better, I realized that all people have real problems. The non-Christian, like the Christian, will try not to show his problems, but is always looking for answers. When I've overcome my fear of talking about personal things, I've been really surprised to see how other people are no better off than I am, and that they have a longing, just like the Bible says."

Of course, not everyone sits around and moans about how bad life is. Hardly anyone feels that way all the time. And even when a person does feel low, he usually tries to hide it. In fact, we're all pretty good at putting up that false front. How many people know it when you are doubting? Do you tell everyone about your problems? About your sense of inadequacy? Chances are that sometimes when you're most troubled inside, some kids who know you are thinking, "Man, if only my life could be like that—with no problems!"

It may even be that the guy or gal you look at and envy because he's having such a ball is actually pretty miserable inside. He may even feel like Ronna. ''There are millions and millions of dots, and I feel I should compare myself with them and give you some idea as to my relationship with them. I feel as though I am a common dot. To myself I am special, but I face the fact that every dot must feel he is important. It is the desire of each of us to be accepted as a great guy or real pal, and of course I am no exception. I don the silly clothes, listen to loud blaring music, dance the frantic dances, and laugh even though the joke was not funny. Every one of us seems to be somewhat fake. Surely this must not be too great a sin. Doesn't everyone do these things, or am I the only one?"

Life a ball? It may look like it, but it doesn't necessarily feel that way inside.

"In high school," says a college fellow, "I served as student council president, and worked closely with the 'in' kids—the ones that every teen would like to be like—the popular, content and happy kids. Someone has to let other teens know that even these kids are not happy and content, but are farther away from happiness than anyone else on the social ladder. They are constantly frustrated within themselves."

"I think," says a Pennsylvania seventeen-year-old, "that many kids today are looking for meaning in life— witness marijuana, LSD, free sex, etc." And a Washington teen adds, "I doubted the relevancy of God for a period of several months. But God's reality really hit me when some of my good friends from school got hooked on drugs because they couldn't find answers to life through 'practical' means. It was then that I found God's compassion and understanding to be the *only* practical means."

It is interesting. Why, if life without God is such a ball, do kids try things like drugs? Medical authorities suggest three reasons. To rebel, for kicks, or as a cure-all for troubles. "I first turned on," says a suburban Illinois teen, "at the boarding school my parents sent me to in Wisconsin. It was to escape the terrible boredom I felt at the school and to work out the antagonisms I felt toward my parents.

"We felt we were under a lot of tension and used to worry about whether our parents would still be on our backs when we got out of school. For me, marijuana was emotionally addictive. I needed to escape from things."[2]

Life isn't easy for anyone, believer or unbeliever. Life jolts us all. Not just with the big showy things, but with hidden things inside. With worry. About school. About parents. About friends. About our future, our failings, our panic as things pile up.

Some turn to drugs to carry them through. Some turn to God. "The thing that convinced me of God's existence," says a Missouri girl, "is answered prayer. This college load is more than I'd figured on. I have faced serious psychological depressions and physical fatigue, and have considered crashing through the window of a lounge on the fifth floor of the dorm to end it all. Yet I prayed that God would pick me up and carry me through, and I've been amazed at the way He's lifted my spirits and completely changed my attitudes. I know I can handle it all now, but only with the help of God. He's for real."

Now, this testimony doesn't "prove" God. Of course not. It *could* be all psychological. The power of positive thinking. But the point is, Christian and non-Christian both experience a real sense of need. Each faces pressures. Each is aware, at some time or other, that something is lacking in his life.

Now, the grass may be greener on the other side of the fence of faith. But it's not greener because life there is just a big ball. It's not greener because over there life is a way-out trip of carefree joy. Life is life. And life just isn't a ball.

Life, real life, makes all of us aware that we need—something.

Might be, probably is, but—

That's the way one teen sees it. "God might be real,

probably is. It's just that it's hard to really believe He acts in people today. The 'Christian' kids are kind of fundies sometimes. Some are really neat. But I don't know if God is real or just an idea in their minds."

Certainly just because we'd *like* to believe in God, or *like* to feel like the kids who say God helps them, we have no reason to believe that He really exists. It may be, as our friend above wonders, "just an idea in their mind." "In this intellectual world," says an Oklahoma eighteen-year-old, "a teenager needs *very* badly to have security in knowing that his basic Christian ideas are really true." It's not enough for any honest person to have a faith that's like Linus' blanket! It's got to be *real*.

And this creates a problem. Real, hard evidence of God and of His working in daily life seems hard to find. The gospel, says the New Testament, "seems foolish to the Jews because they want a sign from heaven as proof that what is preached is true; and it is foolish to the Gentiles because they only believe what agrees with their science and seems wise to them" (1 Cor. 1:22). People like these, who look for tangible, physical, visible evidence regularly pass God off as foolishness. There just doesn't seem to be evidence that would satisfy people like this.

But isn't there any evidence? "I think," says an Illinois sixteen-year-old, "that kids and people in general doubt the existence of God because He is an intangible in a tangible world. One can see an intangible such as love at work in such things as a husband-wife relationship and parent-child relationship. Therefore a teen generally accepts love as a reality. But it is hard for a teen to see the ways God moves and works in our world."

Intangibles *are* real. We can see their effect in our world and in our lives. And, remember, everyone who has any sophisticated view of "God" tends to view Him the same way. As real, but intangible. As real, but not in the same way that the material universe is "real." As the Bible puts it, "God is Spirit."

Now, if God is real and intangible, it may well be that His primary ways of working in our world are intangible.

That is, God doesn't appear on mountaintops anymore, and He doesn't talk to us over TV. He doesn't materialize a club and hit us when we sin. If He is responsible for current events and our daily experiences, as He well may be, we have no way of tracing the responsibility back to Him. So it may be helpful to look for *intangible* evidence. To see if there is any hint that God is at work in an intangible way in our tangible world.

This is a problem people have faced before. Habakkuk, over six hundred years before Christ, looked at the moral mess his nation was in and cried to God,

> Oh Jehovah! How long must I cry for help,
>   and you not respond?
> I cry to you of violence, yet you do not deliver.
> Why do you make me constantly gaze on wickedness?
>   you yourself endure the sight of mistreatment?
> Havoc and violence are before me,
>   causing strife and contention to arise.
> In this situation law is benumbed,
>   justice ever absent,
>   for with the wicked overwhelming the righteous
>   perverted justice is administered.
>   Habakkuk 1:2-4 (free trans.)

God answered, as recorded in the book, that He wasn't just standing by. He was raising up a fierce people to bring the judgment of war and defeat on the sinning nation. But this got Habakkuk even more upset. He felt the victors were worse than the victims! And he wondered, How could God let them get away with it?

That's a question that's bothering a lot of kids today.

We saw it earlier in this chapter. "How come they have such a good time?" "How come he gets away with cheating all the time, and I try it just once and get caught?" "How come the non-Christian has it so much better? Better clothes. And prettier girls. How come?"

And sometimes they do! So we wonder. How *can* God let them get away with it?

But when Habakkuk recorded God's answer to his question he said something about our question too. He said something about intangibles.

"Look!" the Habakkuk passage says, pointing to the person who "has everything."

> Look! He is swelled with pride,
>   His inmost soul is perverted.
> Indeed, this wine is heady!
>   The haughty hero will never be at rest!
>   He who has magnified himself
>   is like hell—
>   he is like death—
>   He will never be satisfied
>   He will keep on gathering all the nations,
>   keep on assembling all the peoples
>   to himself.
>   Habakkuk 2:5 (free trans.)

See it? "Getting away with it" goes to your head. It puffs you up. And when you magnify yourself, and push your desires and wants, it's "like hell, like death." How? Neither can be filled up. You keep on getting more, *but you can't be satisfied.*

It's funny. Here's a guy who's going to make that million, and then retire. And when he gets it? He goes after another. Somehow, it didn't satisfy. In fact, getting what he thought he wanted only increased his desire. It made him *want* more.

Now, if there really is a God and, as Christians believe,

we need Him to satisfy us, isn't this about the way things should work? Wouldn't He build into the human personality a sense of emptiness, of dissatisfaction, that only He could fill? That no substitute we could try would do?

Well?

What's the last thing you wanted desperately? That was going to really satisfy you? Did you get it?

Are you satisfied now?

Life, real life, makes all of us aware that we need—something. And maybe there's a reason.

Now, there's nothing *conclusive* about any of these things. It may be interesting to think of doubts and pressures and emptiness in our lives as pointers to something real "out there" that is waiting to fill the gap. It is suggestive that this yearning all of us seem to experience "fits" the Christian idea of God. But, of course, it's possible that we've invented a God to fill the gap, not that God shaped the gap to point us to Him. "God" may be a wish fulfillment demanded by the fact of our finiteness.

But there are other intangibles, other gaps, that can't be explained quite that way. Some features of human personality are almost inexplicable. And one of them has to do with our sense of morality.

C. S. Lewis puts it this way: "There are two points I wanted to make. First, that human beings, all over the earth, have this curious idea that they ought to behave in a certain way, and cannot really get rid of it. Secondly, that they do not in fact behave that way. They know the Law of Nature; they break it. These two facts are the foundation of all clear thinking about ourselves and the universe we live in."[3]

What does Lewis mean, that these facts are the basis of all clear thinking about ourselves and the universe we live in?

He means that whatever else we say about the nature of man, we are the only life on earth that has a sense of responsibility to do something other than follow our impulses. We have the idea that we ought to order our lives by concepts of right and wrong, even when these block fulfillment of our desires! And, strangely, we're all aware that we don't behave the way we think we ought to.

We must, says Lewis, begin to understand ourselves by seeing what this fact means to us.

And the universe? That somehow it's a moral universe. That right and wrong really exist.

Now, this is a rather unpopular view. It's clear that different civilizations have different standards of right and wrong. That moral codes differ. And that the moral code we happen to hold is one that was taught us by our parents and our culture. So why should we go outside of culture and talk about a "moral universe"? Why not just think of morality as a cultural invention?

For one thing, morality is universal. Every culture, every society, has a moral code. Lots of cultures have gotten along without the wheel, or the steam engine. But none have gotten along without moral codes. Even the "differences" between cultural codes aren't so great as is sometimes made out. OK, so one culture says you can have four wives, and another says you can have only one. But none says you can have any woman you want! One group says it's fair to cheat in business deals; another says you have to be scrupulously honest. But each group has the idea of "it's fair." And each has the idea of "cheat" and "honest."

We even look at the moral codes of different cultures and say that one is "better" than the other. We don't say that we "like" American values and "dislike" Nazi values. We say that one is better. And in making this statement we're saying that we really believe that right and wrong exist. And that the one system is closer to right than the other. We're saying that somehow, outside of cultures and judging cultures, there is a real right and a real wrong.

We may say we don't believe there is a real right or a real wrong. But we do. We believe in it so much that when we do a thing we think is wrong, we immediately start making excuses for ourselves. "He deserved it." "It was only a little peek, and I could almost remember the answer anyway." "My folks are really better off thinking I'm going to Jan's, so it's better I told them that little lie. Now they won't worry."

As Lewis says, all this is "one more proof of how deeply, whether we like it or not, we believe in the Law of Nature. The truth is, we believe in decency so much—we feel the Rule of Law pressing on us so—that we cannot bear to face the fact that we are breaking it, and consequently try to shift responsibility. For you notice that it is only for our bad behavior that we find all these explanations. It is only our bad temper that we put down to being tired or worried or hungry; we put our good temper down to ourselves."[4]

And this happens *everywhere*. To everyone.

It almost seems that some component of the human personality is broken or burned out. We can sense right, but so often we don't do it. And it's interesting that the Bible says of other cultures, "Even though they never had God's written laws . . . down in their heart they knew right from wrong. God's laws are written within them; their own conscience accuses or sometimes excuses them. They know what is right, but don't do it" (Rom. 2:12-15).

And the thought of God, in this situation, isn't comforting! Because we've got the idea that God, who put the moral ideas in us in the first place, isn't pleased if we violate His code. That's why we make excuses. To avoid blame. And we feel that God *is* blaming us.

I can see how we might invent the idea of God to fill our emptinesses. But who'd invent God to torment him about his failings?

So, how about this intangible? How about this gap— the gap that exists in all of us between the right we know, and the wrong we do? How about the excuses we all make for behavior we know isn't right?

How do we explain it?

If right and wrong are simply cultural, why is morality universal? Why is it a basic element in human nature?

If right and wrong are unreal, why is our awareness that we've failed so great when we do something wrong? Why can't we just pass it off as unimportant? Where did that awful, demanding, accusing knowledge of right come from?

Somehow such intangibles—things we can't touch and measure and weigh—are still very real to us. Such intangibles, while they don't "prove" God exists, do fit in with how things would be if God did exist, and if He were necessary.

For, if there really is an emptiness in our lives that only God can fill, our experience is telling us that God is necessary!

If there really is a burned out or broken component in our personality that turns us away from the right we know we ought to do, and if God can fix it and fix us, He's necessary.

If God can do these things in our life, we'd be a long way toward that "new and different person with a fresh newness in all you do and think" that the Bible talks about (Rom. 12:2).

The grass on the other side of *that* fence sure would be greener!

Steps to take

1. What, besides God, might explain the "intangibles" the author talks about in this chapter? What do you think is the percentage chance for each of being the right explanation?

2. What do you think of the idea of "intangible evidence" for God? Have you experienced these empty feelings yourself?

3. There's a book in the Bible that gives an insight into a person who looks for meaning in life apart from God. It's Ecclesiastes. Why not read it, and see if it says what you sometimes feel?

3

On our own

"There are times when things are going really well," says an Illinois girl, "and if life doesn't seem essentially beautiful at least it's liveable. Things go well, problems don't arise (for a while at least), and at times like these it's not that I actively think of God as not necessary, but I seem to be doing well enough on my own so I don't have to depend on Him. He isn't necessary to me right then."

She's like a lot of us. We're not racked up all the time. Things go well. And it's pretty clear that usually we can do well enough—

I spent an hour or so with some high school kids in Kalamazoo, Michigan, a couple of months ago. I asked them, "When, from your own experience, do you think people get the feeling that God isn't really necessary?" Here's what a few of them said:

"I get carried away with everything when things are going good for me. Sometimes I think prayer helps; but most of the time when things are going good, I don't think of Him as much as I should."

"When classes are going smoothly and the social life is swinging, the presence of God is taken for granted and, in essence, forgotten; not necessarily intentionally, but forgotten. A bad quiz or a 'bad trip' (so to speak) brings it all home again and sobers you up."

"It seems, at times, that anything and everything will happen anyway whether you pray or not. So God may seem very unnecessary and a waste of time."

"This is usually when you're feeling real good, sort of in a euphoria. You think that if everything is going so well, why should you have a God. I really don't know what helps, or maybe I should say I don't think anything helps. Just because you feel good, I don't think you should all of a sudden stop and pull out your Bible or pray."

All this squares with what the other kids who wrote me had to say. That much of the time it's hard to see how God fits into life. *How* do we need Him? Where is He experienced? "If only," one fellow wrote, "a teenager had the experience of praying and having that prayer answered or was in a situation where prayer was really necessary as a daily part of life, then God would seem more necessary."

Sometimes, and to some kids, prayer does seem a necessary part of life. "I have almost always made 'A's' on my report card," says a young Kansas girl. "In the lower grades it was easy to make good grades, but I found that if I didn't ask God to help me when I went to study for a test I didn't remember what I was supposed to learn. But if before I even opened my books, I prayed and asked God to help me I made a good grade. This is not an earthshaking experience, but it is something that would help a lot of teenagers if they would only tune in on God. I found that God is relevant even in what we consider very small, unimportant matters."

Or take this word from a fourteen-year-old. "Popularity

is an area in which I have thought that I didn't need God
in. I always wanted to be 'in.' But most of the time I was
out, because people knew I was supposed to have been a
Christian but I wasn't living it. I have realized (with
God's help) that no matter how hard you try that not
everyone will like you. I have also learned it is hard to like
everyone else. But with God's help you can accomplish
more. So you can see the need for God."

Maybe. But these two incidents aren't likely to convince
many. After all, how many kids get A's and *don't* pray
before they study? How many kids have struggled to be
"in" and, for one reason or other (without God's help),
found ways to adjust? Wouldn't it be fair for them to
testify that they *don't* need God or prayer? Wouldn't it be
fair for them to say, "If 'God' and prayer help you, fine.
You do your thing. But let me do mine!"

Tie the need for God to things like grades and popularity, or any of the hundreds of other lumps and bumps you
hit in the high school and college years, and the idea that
God is *necessary* isn't too convincing. Helpful, maybe.
But *necessary*? Unlikely.

To be really honest, we ought to admit that the pre-
scription for good grades is study, not prayer. Try not
cracking a book and then pray all night before the term
test, and see how well you do! And the way to be popular
is to be friendly. And the way to succeed in business?
Work hard or marry the boss' daughter.

Just take an honest look around. Look at the people who
are successful, the ones who really accomplish things. Did
Einstein have to be a Christian to become a great
mathematician? Or did the Beatles have to be believers to
be good musicians? Or Ph.D.'s, to be smart? Or do the
sharp kids and adults you know have to be Christians to
be respected and looked up to?

Switch worlds

Of course not. And most scientific, material and cultural advances today aren't the product of Christians who produce in reliance on God. They're the product of men and women who use their minds and wills and talents that nature or God gave them, and who've "made it" strictly on their own.

So the guy who wrote, "I can do pretty well on my own. I'm independent," was probably right. In our kind of world a person can make out pretty well on his own. Not everyone does. But we *can*.

No wonder a lot of teens and those in their twenties see only a "bland, casual need for God; the kind of necessary on Sunday, but useless during the week" faith.

You may have noticed it, maybe not. But we *have*

switched worlds. In the last chapter we started talking about the intangible world we're all a part of, and suggested that we can most easily track God down by examining that world. *But the fellows and girls quoted in this chapter have been looking for God in the tangible world!* The world of tests and popularity. And that's the world where—if God *is* at work—it's harder to trace things directly back to Him.

So often the issue is confused. So often the "Christian life" is confused with little lists of dos and don'ts that any hypocrite can follow. "One honest reason for honest doubts," says a New York senior, "is that the person is misinformed. He thinks Christianity is just to be good and all. Naturally he sees no reason to become involved when he can 'be good' without church help."

According to an Illinois college girl, "The biggest problem for me has been my parents and my church forcing a Christianity on me that just doesn't agree with what Christ advocated. The most important thing for a Christian is to love God and his brother. It's no wonder Christianity has a bad sound, when all we see is negative: don't smoke, drink, play cards, dance, go to movies, etc. It's no good at all if you don't love."

When we say, "It's no good at all if you don't love," we're getting back into the area of the intangibles—where the issue really belongs. For the sure marks of a person whose life God has actually touched won't be found in the lists he follows. They'll be found on the inside. "Now," the Bible puts it, "your attitudes and thoughts must all be constantly changing for the better. Yes, you must be a new and different person, holy and good" (Eph. 4:23-24).

But it's just at this point, where we recognize the need

for a drastic inner change from jealousy and envy to love
and compassion, that we discover that *we're* no good
at all.

The gap revisited

People can get along without God in most things. But
there are some ways it seems people can't. And it's in
these areas we ought to explore to see if God perhaps is,
and if He can be experienced.

In the last chapter I suggested that one of the intangibles that "fits" the Christian way of looking at reality is
the gap that exists between what we feel we *ought* to do
and what we actually do. Between what we feel we ought
to be, and what we are.

Now, there's no doubt that this gap exists. No matter
what you believe about God. As Harvard's Dr. Graham
Blaine says, "The nature of man, whether viewed in religious or psychiatric terms, makes it difficult for him to
control himself and behave in a way that appears rational
and reasonable from his own as well as society's point of
view. He needs help, sometimes simply as an ordinary
citizen trying to go about his business in a sensible fash-
ion, and sometimes as a patient crippled by neurotic
symptoms. He looks outside himself for assistance in
controlling his impulses, strengthening his will, sorting
out what is real from what is imagined, and gaining perspective on life as a whole, in terms of meaning and purpose and what his own individual goals and ambitions
should be." And yet, Dr. Blaine points out, irrational
forces inside seem to "compel one to behave in a manner
contrary to one's better judgment."[1]

We don't have to go far to find that this is the way
things really are. We *don't* control ourselves, and do
what's right. Not that we're terribly concerned about it.

Recently seventy-five percent of those who responded to a public opinion poll asking if people are "generally getting better or worse morally" said people are getting worse. Yet seventy-five percent on the same poll rated *themselves* as "morally adequate." We can see things so easily in others; so poorly in ourselves.

For instance, one of the things your generation is so critical of is hypocrisy and phoniness in the older generation. But that works both ways. Jacques Barzun, in *The American University*, writes, "The prevalence of cheating is but the most obvious example of what a jargoneer would call the 'morality gap.' Students expect honesty and truthfulness from teachers and administration but not from themselves. To cheat or not to cheat is an open question discussed in college newspapers throughout the country. Plagiarism in term papers, senior theses, and Ph.D. dissertations has naturally grown with the growth of cheaters. Not all of them go so far as to obtain their pocket money by stealing books from the college book store, but that practice too has become at least an available way of life."[2]

Sure, cheating is wrong. But most kids cheat a little or a lot. Chances are you have too. Not long ago a professor at an evangelical college asked if students had done required reading. When their written responses were compared with library cards, it was clear *many* hadn't—and had lied.[3] I'm sure that in just a few short moments you could take a pencil and paper and jot down a half-dozen things you've done *this week* that you feel sure were wrong. Just a very little honesty and you'll discover a "morality gap" in *your* life, just as there's one in mine and every other person's in the world.

Now, before you get me wrong, let me say that I'm not busy trying to get you to say you're a "sinner." Or suggesting that you ought to. Or that I'm deliberately trying to make you feel guilty.

Maybe you do feel guilty about something just now. OK. But if you don't, please don't try to inject a shot of artificial guilt feelings. Sure, if the Christian gospel is true, whether you feel it or not, you *are* guilty for doing what you know is wrong. That's "a sin," and the Bible says, "He will punish sin, wherever it is found" (Rom. 2:12). But, remember, at this point we're not ready to say the Christian gospel is true. It's just one option.

Why all this bit about the morality gap then?

Because whatever it means, *the gap is there*. And if we're really understanding ourselves we need to explore it.

In talking about a "sense of sin" J. B. Phillips suggests we shouldn't "get melodramatic or morbid or self-pitying about it. If you begin to follow God instead of going your own sweet way there's bound to be a moment—and probably more than one—when you feel cheap and nasty. Don't worry, that's a healthy sign. It means you're beginning to touch reality."[4]

What he's saying is that the "sense of sin" is a clue to who you really are. To what you're really like. That when you get over the preoccupation with lists, and buckle down to try to do what you know is right, you're hit in the face with the awareness that something is wrong. That you've got a *need*. That, on your own, here's one thing you just *can't* do.

And this is important. It's rather silly to point to all the things we *can* do (like pass quizzes) as evidence that God isn't necessary. That's something like a baby sneering at the need to grow up, because maturity isn't necessary for him to toddle across the floor! A person needs to grow up because of all the things he *can't* do without maturity; not because of the things he can do. And if God is necessary to us, we ought to find it out by looking at the things we can't do without Him; not the things we can.

Now, in this chapter and the last I've suggested that, from the Christian perspective, there are at least two things we can't do without God. Both are intangible, but very real. These two things are (1) be truly satisfied, and (2) be truly good people. You might take a lifetime to find out that first one. Or you might learn it now by noting that even when you get what you want, you really aren't satisfied. But the second thing is easy to prove.

How? Honestly try to follow the law the Bible says God put in your heart. Try to do, *always,* what you believe and know is right. Or, if you want to make the test a little tougher (and the need a little clearer) try to follow in the footsteps of Jesus. Read the Gospels; then try to be like Him.

Try to follow that call, and you'll soon find out that you are, in fact, a sinner. That you truly can't be "good."

This, by the way, is the only way to find out. I can't *force* the Christian viewpoint on you. I'm not even trying. I'm certainly not going to thunder at you that you're a sinner.

That's something you've got to find out for yourself.

And, if you try to, you will.

God at work?

It's suggestive anyway. If God were real, could He have chosen a better way to shout at us than through these intangibles?

Can't you just see it? There's a man who has everything: unhappy, unsatisfied, yearning for something else. And there's a man who's honestly tried to do the right but runs up against failure after failure, deeply troubled about himself. And there's God, standing in the wings. Ready to walk on and meet each need. Just waiting till we busy people turn away from our tangible baubles and are willing to see Him.

Now, maybe this isn't the way it is.

But maybe it is.

And if it is, it's something you can *experience*.

Some kids claim they have experienced it: both the emptiness and the filling.

"There used to be many times when I really wondered if there was a God," says a seventeen-year-old Minnesota coed. "And if there was one, what did He have to do with me. This all came to a crisis one day when I realized that I didn't really care about religion and I would put on a false front every time I stepped into church.

"That day I went to the Bible and read many verses where it tells about God—His strength, existence, characteristics, and purpose. This convinced me that God is very much alive and is necessary in everyone's life. But since that time, I wondered if I needed God when I would get good grades on tests, etc., in school without even praying for God's help. But after a jolting, yet minor experience with God, I knew I need Him *always* in *everything*. I feel every Christian goes through experiences such as this when he doubts God. This is all part of the growing process."

And remember Judy from chapter 1? "I honestly realized I had nothing. I had no purpose in life, no reason for being a Christian—my life was a mess and I was desperate." Later she wrote, "As I look back, I am extremely thankful for this period in my life. It was actually an introduction to a vital relationship with my Lord. I now have a relationship with Him that I would not have believed possible a year ago."

"It's tough living with yourself," one fellow wrote,

"especially when you don't measure up to what you think you should." But, responds another, "I finally realized my need for Christ, and then things began to click."

Kind of funny, isn't it?

To think that maybe the troubles, the dissatisfactions, the very things that make us doubt, are possibly evidence that God cares? That He exists? That He *is* working in our lives?

We're so stuck on the tangible world. We think of God working in our lives in terms of the things we want, not the things we don't want.

The Bible doesn't picture it that way. "For God sometimes uses sorrow in our lives," writes Paul, "to help us turn away from sin and seek eternal life. We should never regret his sending it" (2 Cor. 7:10).

And James even says, "Let there be sorrow and sincere grief. Let there be sadness instead of laughter and gloom instead of joy. Then when you feel your worthlessness before the Lord, he will lift you up, encourage and help you" (James 4:9-10).

Now, don't get the picture of God as a big tyrant. These verses don't suggest that God gets a kick out of our suffering or abasement. They just reflect the way the Bible says things really are. The way we are. It may hurt to face the intangibles; but as long as we think we're getting along OK on our own, we're not likely to look for God. As long as we think we're the big success, we're not likely to discover that really we're sinners. We can see right, but not do it. And we can never become the kind of persons we really want to be.

It's then that we're ready to listen to what God says He can, and must, do for us. And that is to change us completely. "When someone becomes a Christian," says the Bible, "he becomes a brand new person inside. He is not

the same any more. A new life has begun" (2 Cor. 5:17).
And for something like this—a new life—God certainly is
necessary.

Now, again, none of this proves God.

But it does suggest a way that we can "prove" Him for
ourselves.

And proving God this way, in experience, begins with
an awareness of our need. With testing the intangibles.
And discovering that while there are some things we *can*
do, the biggest things of all we simply can't.

Not on our own.

Steps to take

1. Where are you, now? Which of the following
   quotes is you?
   a. "I can do pretty well on my own."
   b. "I'm caught up in frustrations and dissatisfac-
      tion."
   c. "I don't measure up to what I think I should."
   d. "I know have a relationship with Him I
      wouldn't have believed possible a year ago."

2. The author suggests that, if God really is, He is
   necessary in at least two areas. What are these
   areas? How could you prove or disprove this in
   your life?

3. Do you think you ought to expect God to work in
   your daily life? How?

4

G-O-D Who?

"I had doubt of the worthiness of God," says a New Jersey high school junior, "when I had a very close member of my family die. I felt that God was being unmerciful and unjust."

When we look at the things that happen to us, we can get a lot of different ideas of what God might be like. And that's one of the problems. Even if evidence "in here" points to a real God "out there," we still have to struggle with the question of what "God" might be like!

The words came hesitantly at first. And then they began to pour out. God was so unfair. And all the things he'd been taught, and things he'd even taught others, just weren't true.

What was wrong with this college sophomore, son of missionary parents? The main thing, the thing it all seemed to hinge on, was his fear that perhaps God wanted *him* on the mission field. And, whatever he did in life, my friend did not want to go to the mission field.

Yet he had the terrible conviction that he'd have to go there anyway.

"What's the use?" he was saying. "It doesn't make any difference what *I* want. He'll make me do what He wants in the end anyway. What's the use of planning my life or of wanting anything? No matter what I plan, no matter what I want, I'm going to be forced to do it His way.

"How can there be any freedom? Who wants to be a puppet, pushed around with nothing to say about his life?

"Why can't I have something to say about my own life?"

It's kind of scary when you think of it that way.

Does God being "out there" rob us of something important? Does it mean we're not respon-

sible anymore? That we may *think* we make choices, but that we're really being jerked along by hidden strings? Is *that* the kind of God who's really out there, waiting for us to stumble into Him?

This is one of the biggest problems we have when we begin to face those intangibles that point us toward God. Do we want to go on? A look inside ourselves might suggest that God is real, and that He's left His footprints all across our personalities. But those footprints aren't God. Seeing them doesn't tell us much about what God is really like.

And we've all got a lot of mixed-up ideas about God.

What's God like?

I asked a number of teens and those in their twenties to tell me what picture they think their friends have of God. And I got a number of very interesting images. Most of them portray a God I surely wouldn't want to meet on a dark night!

What were some of them? Here are the most common:

The Rule-maker God. According to this picture, God spends most of His time observing to see what's fun for us, and then making a rule against it. To lots of kids, God could be replaced by a STOP sign.

Usually the rules He makes are annoying, but rather irrelevant. "Many of my friends doubt the relevance of God," says an Illinois twenty-one-year-old. "Why should they believe in God? They don't see Him working in Christians' lives—they almost see a degree of nonsense in those that are Christians. For example, Christians aren't supposed to dance, drink, smoke, play cards, etc." And a Colorado girl agrees. "Most kids think Christianity is a set of 'don'ts!' They doubt there's any real value in it since they see adults breaking these don'ts, and nullifying their own religion."

Is *that* God? Spending His time piddling around with playing cards while there's suffering and human need all around us?

The Policeman God. According to this image, God is always running around waiting to blow the whistle and club you. His main interest is sin, and He likes nothing better than to observe a juicy one and write you up a ticket on it.

One of His favorite pastimes when He's off duty is to remind you of what you've done and make you feel guilty. He really gets a kick out of that. That way you suffer twice for your sins: now by feeling the guilt, and later by feeling the fire.

The Sissy God. This God is a rather doddering Grandfather, a kind old Being "who helps people who are in trouble and comforts old people when they are dying."

He's a rather popular God, and very concerned about the public opinion polls. He never does anything that would offend anyone, or takes any strong stand, but sits there oozing a rather sticky brand of "love." One of the reasons He's so popular is that He never bothers anyone; and no matter what you do, He likes nothing better than to pass out cookies. He's got all the character of a marshmallow, and is awfully pleased if you get around to church twice a year to nod to Him.

The Merchant God. This God is all business. He sits there keeping a sharp set of books and weighing all your acts on a scale. And, buddy, you'd better keep on the credit side of His ledger.

"It used to seem like I was always trying to please Him, and I thought He wasn't concerned with me but only with what I did for Him," says a teen who knew the Merchant

God intimately. To Him we're all on a production line of "good works" or of "spiritual activities" and we have to dig in to produce our quota. And watch that ten percent of the gross. It comes off the top, or He's likely to foreclose on our prosperity.

The Sovereign Tyrant. This God struts around His private palace grounds, and all us peons have to fall flat on our faces anytime His shadow is within ten miles. Sometimes, for His amusement, He sets us up on His chessboard and plays a game with our lives. (This is especially the fate waiting for anyone who tries to get brownie points by offering Him full control.) As one teen says, this God is a "dictator who, if He was given full control of our lives would lead us through a miserable life of self-sacrifice."

With this God none of us count for anything. In fact, the whole bundle of us wouldn't add up to zero. If He wasn't amused by having us around, He'd brush us all off just like that.

The Force. This God is a very distant, very impersonal "it." And so He's quite unimportant and indefinite. The main thing about this God is His unhumanity. He's not even inhuman. He's so different, so "far out," that we can't even talk meaningfully about Him.

The Force may push us around, but it's not from meanness. He probably doesn't even know we're in the way. So we just live with Him, and if we get run over at least it's with no more malice than if it were by a runaway bulldozer.

This God used to go around under the name "Fate," but we got to be more scientific and gave Him an up-to-date name.

He doesn't mind. He didn't even notice.

And there are others. Lots of other ideas of what God is

like. Lots of images that characterize Him, and try to help us grasp the shadowy shape the intangibles point us to.

The trouble is, these ideas are all wrong.

How do we know they're wrong? There are several ways of knowing.

One way we know these images of God are wrong is by noting that we know where these images came from. They're all hangovers from childhood. For instance, take the Great God STOP. Some friends have a three-year-old who was told in Sunday school that "Jesus always sees us." During the following week she came into the house one day and complained furiously to her mother, "I wish He'd leave me alone! I wish He'd leave me alone!" Mother thought a neighbor boy had been annoying the girl and went out to chase him away. But there was no one there. And then the tot explained, "I wanted to pick some flowers, but Jesus was watching. I wish He'd leave me alone!"

You see?

Our image of God isn't shaped so much by what we're told about Him, but *by how the idea of God has functioned in our experiences.* If God's omnipresence was sensed as a barrier to doing what we wanted, we began to picture Him as a killjoy. As a STOP sign. And later on if "God" was used by our parents or our church to enforce behavior patterns, the idea was confirmed. Soon we began to think about God Himself, not as He is, but as He has been used by others to shape our behavior.

The same thing goes for the other false ideas. If mom and dad loved us conditionally, only expressing approval when we performed satisfactorily, soon we built up a picture of the Merchant God. If "God" was used as a club to make us obey, we got the picture of the Sovereign Tyrant.

Gods that have so clearly been made in the image of our frustrations are not likely to accurately reflect the real God.

Another way we know these images of God are false is by noting that each of them is "mean"—belittling. These are characteristics we dislike in people! Why, we haven't even shaped these "gods" after the good qualities we can observe—love, and kindness, and self-sacrifice. We've chosen the worst. The qualities that all of us would rightly label "bad."

And this just can't be. Why? Well, remember, we've already shown that this is a moral universe. That somehow there is implanted in us an idea of right, of good. And if we're right in thinking that it's God who has made us moral beings, *He simply could not be immoral Himself!*

So these ideas of God that make us fear and cringe and dislike Him just have to be false ideas. And the gods that we create have to be false gods.

If God is real, finding Him isn't such a risk as we sometimes make out.

Breakthrough

Now, again, we're left with more questions than answers and no hard information about God to prove them.

In the first three chapters all we've done is try to see if it makes sense to ask for evidence of God's existence. Some people seem to sniff around the tangible world for His tracks, and listen to others who shout, "Look! There He goes!" But when we look, we have to say, "Where? I can't see Him."

I've suggested that maybe God has been here all along, looking over your shoulder. Maybe if you glance at the intangible world you'll find He's been right beside you!

Still, seeing evidence of God isn't seeing God. And

when we look in the intangible world for God Himself, not just for His footprints, we don't get very far.

We could, perhaps, say some things about Him. Somehow He completes our personalities. He fills the gap. He satisfies. And He is a Person, for a *thing* has no concern with morals. Moral action requires choice, and only a person can choose between right and wrong. We might even say that God is a moral Person. If He is the Author of the moral law, then it must reflect His character.

But we can't go much beyond this. Is God nice? Would we like Him? Does He like us? That's hard to say. In fact, when you look at the mess the world is in, and the suffering that occurs daily, you might even conclude that God is a bit of a sadist!

No, seeing God's tracks isn't seeing God. For that, there would have to be some sort of breakthrough by God into the tangible world.

It's here that we run into a peculiar claim of Christianity. The claim that God has done just this: broken through into the tangible world of space and time and history, and broken through in such a way that we can see Him and know Him.

The primary breakthrough, the Christian claims, is Jesus Christ. God "became a human being and lived here on earth among us and was full of loving forgiveness and truth" (John 1:14). And Jesus says, "Anyone who has seen me has seen the Father" (John 14:9).

The Christian also claims that there has been another breakthrough. The Bible. Information passed from beyond the wall of the intangible through men that God guided to write His words. And that these words tell us about God and interpret the world we live in, showing us just how He works in the tangible as well as intangible universe.

Now, we're certainly not ready yet to buy these claims. But we should recognize this: if we are ever going to know God, certainly He must take the initiative. We can't break through into the world of the intangible. We may see His tracks, but we can't, so to speak, "catch Him in the act." We've got no movies or still photos of Him. *Apollo* didn't discover Him crouching on the far side of the moon. So, since we can't break through to Him, He has to break through to us.

We're going to take a hard look at these claims of breakthrough in another chapter. But for now it might be interesting to compare the image of God we get from the Bible with those images of the false gods we saw earlier.

Take the Rule-maker God. The One so worried about the little rules and observances. "Since . . . Christ . . . has set you free from following the world's idea of being saved by certain rules . . ." the Bible says, "why do you keep right on following it anyway, still bound by such rules as not eating, tasting, or even touching certain foods? Such rules are mere human teachings, for food was made to be eaten and used up. These rules may seem good, for rules of this kind require strong devotion and are humiliating and hard on the body, but they have no effect when it comes to conquering a person's evil thoughts and desires. They only make him proud" (Col. 2:20-23).

So, to the God of the Bible, rules for rules' sake are worse than useless. They only make us proud. What does He care about? "Don't criticize each other any more. Try instead to live in such a way that you will never make your brother stumble by letting him see you doing something he thinks is wrong. For after all, the important thing for us as Christians is not what we eat or drink but stir-

ring up goodness and peace and joy from the Holy Spirit"
(Rom. 14:13, 17).

Any rules the real God makes (and He does make some)
are important ones. But who has to be afraid of a *loving*
Rule-maker?

How about the Policeman God who likes to make *us*
suffer? Well, according to the Bible the real God "laid
aside his mighty power and glory, taking the disguise of a
slave and becoming like men. And he humbled himself
even further, going so far as to actually die a criminal's
death on a cross" (Phil. 2:7-8). Why? "It was necessary for
Jesus to be like us, his brothers, so that He could be our
merciful and faithful High Priest before God, a Priest who
would be both merciful to us and faithful to God in deal-
ing with the sins of the people. For since he himself has
now been through suffering and temptation, he knows
what it is like when we suffer and are tempted, and he is
wonderfully able to help us." (Heb. 2:17-18).

God *liking* to make us suffer? Getting a kick out of our
sins? Why, "He became a man so that he could take away
our sins" (1 John 3:5), even when that meant maximum
suffering for Him!

We can do the same for each of the other false gods. The
Merchant God? "Even when we are too weak to have any
faith left [and thus there's no return on His investment],
he remains faithful to us and will help us, for he cannot
disown us who are part of himself" (2 Tim. 2:13).

Even the Tyrant God tumbles when compared to the
God of the Bible. Even when He *is* seen as Sovereign over
the tangible, as well as the intangible, universe.

Freedom now?

Now, that's a hard one to swallow. A sovereign God
providing *freedom?* It's especially hard for people like my

friend Rick whom we met at the beginning of the chapter. People who feel that God binds them, and who want to struggle free.

What they don't see is that if they have no sovereign God, they're *really* bound. They can never be free!

What do I mean? Just this: Rick wants, really, a happy and meaningful life work. There's another thing about Rick. When he talked to me he was going with a girl whom he rather wanted to marry, but whom he didn't think God would let him. Now, again, what Rick really wants is a happy married life (as most of us do).

But Rick has a problem. He *thinks* that some job other than missionary service will give him a meaningful life work, and he *thinks* that this particular girl will give him a happy married life. What's his problem? *He doesn't know!*

A Florida fellow sees it like this: "Though I don't wish to limit God to times of decision, I find Him personally concerned then. Since I am a human (fallible) being, I often make mistakes. To make it even worse, I'm fickle! I can't make up my mind. I can't see ahead ten minutes. I have only hindsight. However, God has both hindsight *and* foresight. So, since He knows the way things will work out, why not let Him be instrumental in deciding my course in life?"

See it? With no God, the only way we can make choices is to guess how things will turn out. And we *are* fallible. Yet, we're stuck with the results of our choices. Free? Man, make one wrong choice, one wrong guess, and you may be hung for life!

But with God maybe we have Someone who can see ahead, guide us to the right choices, and then supervise the results.

And that's the way the Bible (that other "break-through") says God works.

The passage is in 1 Peter, and starts off with a quote from the Old Testament. God, it says, watches over His people and sees to it that things work out right for them. He superintends the ends (3:10-12). Because God sovereignly watches over a person who makes right choices, right choices will nearly always work out so you get what you really want (3:13). Once in a great while you can do right, and there'll be an apparently bad result. You'll suffer for it (3:14). Does that mean that God failed to use His sovereignty? No, just the opposite. When something *seems* to go wrong, it's proof positive, if you did what you believed right, that God has a special hand in things. He is going to use your trouble for a particularly good end—for you and everyone concerned (3:15-17)!

The Bible then gives an example of this sort of thing. It points to Christ, who suffered and died though He always did the right thing. And He suffered in place of people who actually deserved it! And that was God at work. After Christ's resurrection we all saw it. We learned that the time of suffering was God's way of bringing us sinners to God, and led to a wonderful return to heaven for Christ (3:18-22). So sovereignty does work out—in the tangible world.

See how sovereignty and freedom go together?

Sovereignty guarantees the good result of right choices. And *freedom* means that we don't have to worry about results when making decisions; we only have to think about the right thing to do. Best of all, we're always free to do the right thing, because we can trust God to take care of results!

Of course, this kind of trust depends on the image you have of God. "I wish," one fellow wrote me, "you could somehow introduce a very human, yet very sovereign Christ, who is approachable, knowable, loving."

And if the real God were like that—personal, deeply concerned with each of us as individuals—then we could rush to meet Him with no hesitation at all!

Steps to take

1. Take a minute to sketch *your* picture of G-O-D. What do you think He's like?

2. Two Bible passages that portray God vividly are Isaiah 40:6-31 and Mark 2. What kind of character sketch could you make from these chapters?

3. If there hasn't been any breakthrough by God from the world of intangibles, how can we get to know him? Any ideas?

4. If there has been a breakthrough, *how could we prove it?*

5

What's real?

"For me," writes a twenty-one-year-old college girl, "the fields of psychology and sociology seem to analyze life rather fully. There is nothing which cannot be interpreted in psychological terms, including God. I see a big gap between the language of psychology and the language of religion. What is sin? Maybe I'm not a sinner, just psychologically mixed up, unbalanced, or ignorant of some principles about people."

Maybe. But then, so must *everyone* else be! No, as far as the intangible world is concerned, God does seem to fit the facts.

But does "God" fit the facts of the tangible world? Isn't there a big question here?

A New Yorker raises the question, "Many kids have honest doubts about Christianity. Possibly because they feel that the new findings in the field of science, and certain theories conflict with what Christianity teaches." A college girl agrees. "I found myself in a position where I was on the defensive against science, and I'm sorry to say

I don't know how or what to answer a few questions that arose, such as how do you account for fossils and cavemen. How did Noah get all the animals on the earth and all foods into the Ark? According to my biology teacher, there were many more animals on the earth than could ever fit into the ark."

"The question should certainly not be avoided," says another New York fellow. "We can't say, as some do, that science and the Bible do not conflict or that the only disagreements occur when science has overstepped its 'bounds.' Between the average evangelical's interpretation of the Bible and modern science there is a very definite disagreement."

And this disagreement does raise a problem.

Look at it this way. In the first part of the book I suggested that if God is real, His reality should be demonstrable. And when we looked at the way things are in the intangible world, we found that the facts do fit the Christian gospel!

But what happens when we look at the *tangible* world? Do the facts here "fit" too?

And the answer we have to give is, no, they don't seem to! That's what a seventeen-year-old California girl means when she writes, "Help us with some answers to come back at our science teachers and theories of evolution." When we compare what science suggests about "the way things are" with what the Bible says about the way things are, we do get conflicting pictures. Which are we to believe? And why?

Sometimes the answer is given that the Bible (God's "Breakthrough Number Two" into the tangible world) is only accurate when it deals with the intangible world. That as far as the tangible world is concerned it has many errors and was never intended to be scientifically accurate. It is true that the Bible isn't a science text. But it does make peculiar claims throughout as to its truth. "The ordinances of the LORD are true," says the Old Testament of itself (Ps. 19:9 RSV), and the New Testament echoes, "Thy word is truth" (John 17:17 RSV). When you get down underneath the Hebrew and Greek words for "true" you have to face the fact that they assert that *what the Bible says is in full harmony with reality.* That the Bible pictures things the way they actually are. And, as philosophy professor Arthur Holmes writes, Christianity's "truth claims extend to all biblical assertions, those concerning God and man, the history of Israel and the historical Incarnation, miraculous events and supernaturalist doctrines."[1]

So we can't wiggle out of the conflict this way. The Bible does claim to give an accurate picture of reality in the *tangible* as well as the intangible world. And this isn't the same as saying, "I like it that way" or "That's the way I feel it." *Truth* means that it fits the facts.

This is exactly what various scientific views claim. That they are "true" if, and because, they fit the facts. For years men believed that the sun moved around the earth. But the view was rejected by later scientists when they discovered that in fact the earth rotates around the sun. And that's what scientists look for: a harmony with reality.

Now, this would be fine if only the scientific view of reality and the biblical view of reality were the same. But they aren't. Science holds out for evolution. The Bible holds out for creation. And so we have to make a choice. A choice between views of reality.

Fact and theory

Sometimes we don't quite understand the relationship between these two. But it's important that we do if we're going to see our way clearly when we think about conflicting "scientific" and biblical views of reality.

What is the relationship between fact and theory? Suppose you see your dad pick up his fishing tackle, go outside and put it in the car, bring his outboard motor from the basement, put that in the trunk, and get in the car to drive off. Where's he going? It's pretty clear, isn't it? He's going fishing.

How did you know? You knew because you *interpreted facts. All you saw* was what he did. Pick up tackle. Put it in car. Bring out motor. Put it in car. Drive off. These actions you observed were the *facts* (the scientific data). Your conclusion about the meaning of the facts was the *theory*. What's important to note about this is that the *fact* and the *theory* involve two completely different orders of things. The facts are real. Real things or, in this case, real actions. They actually happened, and you could observe them. But the theory is mental. The theory is the way you put together and understand and interpret the facts.

The theory was not "real." For "reality" does not extend to theories.

A theory, while not real, will be true or untrue. If it's true it will be in harmony with facts and explain them. It will *fit* reality. And a theory is only true when it actually fits reality this way.

Now, you probably found it easy to connect the data I suggested in this illustration in order to come up with a theory that was true. Dad *did* go fishing! But many times the data isn't clear enough for us to be sure we've constructed a true theory.

For instance, in Figure 2 is a drawing. No, don't look at it now. In Figure 1 is a series of eight dots. If these are connected correctly, they'll let you discover the reality of the drawing in Figure 2. So try connecting them in Figure 1. Then look at Figure 2 and see if your "theory" (the pattern you draw when you connect the dots), based on

Figure 1

the data you have (the dots), is a "true" theory. See if it actually portrays the reality.

How did you connect them? Were you right?

Actually, there are several possible ways to connect the dots. They could have been connected to make an × in a box, or a butterfly shape, or to make two boxes, one inside the other, like those in Figure 3.

Could you tell from the data you had which was the right shape?

Now, this is the exact question we have to ask about both the scientific and biblical views of reality. Can we tell from the data we have which is the true shape of things? Does one or the other theory really fit the facts?

And when we ask this question, we discover the underlying problem concerning all discussions of the tangible world. *No one has enough data to be sure that the way he connects is the right way.* The data doesn't all point in one direction. There is plenty of data that conflicts with the evolutionary explanation of life on earth. And data that apparently conflicts with the biblical picture of God and His creation.

This isn't the usual picture you get in school. Usually evolution is presented as a fact, not as a theory. And conflicting data isn't emphasized. "In my biology class," a California junior says, "my teacher was giving a lesson about evolution and she left it to the class discussion to disprove these theories or to come up with firm examples of the Bible's teachings to make the creation more understandable. I really tried hard to come up with some examples and such, and I did some, but I really was grasping for some good answers."

Some good answers *can* be found, though it's not my purpose to give them here. I'm not primarily concerned with trying to "disprove" evolution at this point. What I am trying to illustrate is simply this: When we look at the conflicts between science and Scripture, we often confuse the issue. We often think we are looking at a conflict between scientific fact and a biblical world view. Actually we are thinking about a conflict between a particular theory or set of theories about reality which have come to be associated with the so-called "scientific viewpoint" and the biblical theory of reality. And it's a very open question as to which theory is right.

The "scientific viewpoint" has not been proven.

A choice?

How do we make a choice? If one theory is just as good as another, how could anyone ever make an intelligent choice?

Actually, this is not what I'm suggesting. Not at all. Because one theory *isn't* "as good" as another. Because we are interested in *truth.* And because one of these is certainly closer to truth—closer to the way things really are—than the other. So a choice between these two views of reality (the evolutionary, which sees man as a product of nature with no eternal destiny, and the biblical, which sees man as the creation of God and each individual personality as having an eternal destiny) must be made. It's important, not only for that eternity the Christian believes exists, but also for right now. "Without God," a Texas collegian suggests, "I'd have to determine my values differently." And he's right. If there were no God, we'd determine a *lot* of things differently than if there were.

So we need to ask, How do we test these theories?

And this isn't an easy question to answer either. Why? Let's look at the ways we might test any theory.

Observe results. Remember the illustration of dad and the fishing equipment? We theorized from the data we

Figure 2

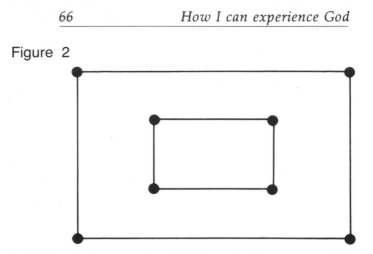

had that dad was going fishing. And we were right. How did we know? Because dad did go fishing.

Figure 3

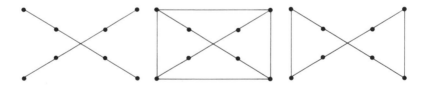

This is one way to test a theory, and a very simple way. Now, says the stock broker, if my theory of market fluctuations is correct, the events of today ought to be reflected by a rise in the market tomorrow. Is his theory right? If the market goes up tomorrow, he's got some evidence that it is. (There may be other factors to explain the rise, so his theory isn't *necessarily* correct—but at least he now has some evidence.) If over a period of time he could call the market rise and fall with 100 percent accuracy, he'd have reason to believe that his theory was true—that it really fit the facts. Because the facts, day after day, fit *it*.

This is a rather hard test to apply to the theories we're talking about. Ultimately the evolutionary will be proven if the world and the universe run down, and man dies out as the stars themselves flicker and dim. Ultimately the biblical will be proven if Christ does come back, and if all are resurrected and stand before God to face His judgment.

But such predictions are themselves unprovable. We can't, now, observe these results. And by the time they do happen, it won't be important anymore. If the evolutionary idea is right, we'll all be dead. If the biblical idea is right, it will be too late. Our destiny will be fixed.

So this approach doesn't seem to hold out much help.

Conduct experiments. This approach is somewhat different, but much like the first. It says that if a theory is right, we should be able to predict that certain things will happen under certain conditions. Then we create those conditions and see if what we thought would happen actually does.

For instance, we have a theory that water will boil at 212 degrees Fahrenheit at sea level. How can I find out if this theory fits the facts? Easily. I just apply heat to water at sea level, and find out. If it does boil, and particularly if I can repeat the experiment over and over again with the same results, I can be sure that the theory is true, that it fits and explains the facts.

In a sense what an experiment does is to go back and *rerun* the event we're considering. Then we watch it and see if it happened the way we thought it did.

But this too is very hard to apply to the theories we're considering. We can't rerun creation—or whatever it was. We can't reproduce the conditions under which the evolutionist thinks life came into being, or the conditions under which he thinks life changed progressively from unicellular to multicellular forms; from tiny cells with no discrete function to complex organisms like man in which many cells have their own unique functions.

So this approach doesn't seem to help much either.

Gather more data. This is another possibility—a far more helpful one. If we can't see results, and prove the theory by watching it work out, and if we can't rerun the events under controlled experimental conditions, we can at least gather more facts and see how they fit the pictures we have of reality. You can see how this works out by thinking back to our eight dots. If there had been just two more dots, some of the possible "real" pictures would have been eliminated!

For instance, if there were two more dots, as in Figure 4, the "real" picture couldn't have been an ×, or an × in a box, or even a butterfly. Additional data cut off several possibilities and pointed clearly toward the shape of the reality the data reflected.

And this is constantly being done by science. New facts are being gathered—by astronomy, by geology, by paleontology, by archeology—from a variety of sciences dedicated to learning and interpreting the data of the tangible

Figure 4

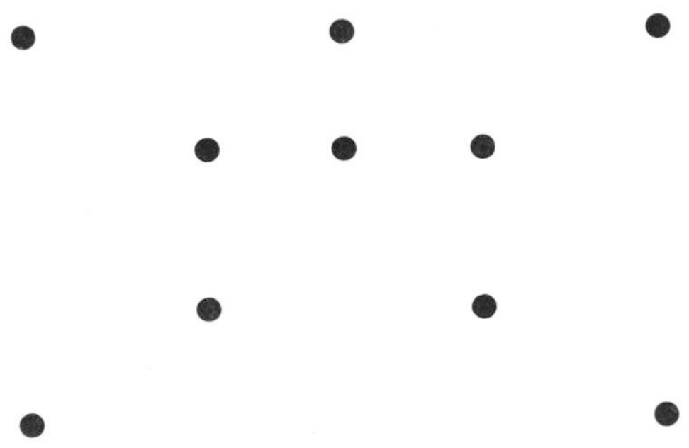

universe. And so the question comes: Does the data really point to either theory? Do we have *enough?*

Here too there's disagreement. Some say, Yes, evolution is now a proven theory. For instance, Sir Julian Huxley asserted at the Darwinian Centennial Convocation at the University of Chicago that "in the evolutionary pattern of thought there is no longer need or room for the supernatural. The earth was not created; it evolved. So did all the animals and plants that inhabit it, including our human selves, mind and soul, as well as brain and body. So did religion."[2] But on the other side, many scientists disagree. Some come out strongly with the denial that the evolutionary "big picture" sketched by Huxley *could* be true. They point to things like the second law of thermodynamics, the question of fitness of the evolutionary environment postulated, closed cycles in the inorganic world, etc.

Even non-Christians writing about evidence offered for the Huxley picture of reality confess, as does Dr. D. Dwight David, that "the facts of paleontology conform equally well with other interpretations"—specifically creation—"and paleontology by itself can neither prove nor refute such ideas."[3]

Boiled down it means simply this: the evidence is not conclusive. The *data* gathered by science fits either picture. The evolutionist interprets it his way; the believer interprets it another way. The data itself does not necessarily rule out either way of thinking.

So in actual fact this approach isn't much help either!

You have to live with one approach to reality or the other. And using just the tangible evidence, the facts and data of science, it's not possible to prove that either view of reality is true. You can't prove "scientifically" what's real.[4]

The hard realities

Some people feel that, even if one can't prove or dis-prove God by what exists in the physical universe, there are plenty of proofs in daily life that God simply cannot exist. The things they point to are the "hard realities" of human life.

Like suffering. A Wyoming girl states the issue like this: "I cringe when people ask, in all earnestness, 'How can I know there's a God?' Because someone is bound to say, 'He's all around. Just look at nature!'

"Well, the truth is that nature is pretty far removed. How many ghetto teens have ever been around 'nature'? Even if they *were* to see it openly, the fact that beauty in nature existed wouldn't account for ugliness, or answer, 'Did God create this mess of slums along with nature?' It's almost as if God had forgotten about the slums to concen-trate on a few little spots of beautiful, rugged wilderness. So, what difference does it make to the individual that God did create beauty? Beauty never caused trouble; it's the ugliness."

Yes, What about the ugliness? What about war? Starva-tion? What about slums and prejudice? What about rob-bery and rape and murder? What about disease—disease that strikes the child and warps his body as well as the adult's?

How do these very real things square with our idea of God: a God who, the Bible says, loves us all?

To many people this is *the* unanswerable argument against God. If God is good, they feel, He wouldn't let such terrible things happen. If God is all-powerful, they add, He could stop them. So, since God doesn't stop them, and since they do exist, there simply cannot be a God like the Christian proclaims. A God who is love, and who is sovereignly powerful in the tangible universe as well.

But this problem is really just like the problem with science. In both cases we have to admit the data. Suffering does exist. *But, again, the data is not in itself the proof.* There is the same kind of leap from the facts to the explanation of the facts we saw with science; from data to theory.

To one group, those who object to God on the basis of suffering, it seems impossible that a good God would permit human agony—at least of the kind that exists. Others, looking from a biblical perspective, do not minimize suffering. But they say that God *has* permitted suffering—and for good!

This, too, is an issue that can't really be settled. It should be clear to everyone that God can work through suffering. He did in the life of Sue, a seventeen-year-old from Pennsylvania. "Until recently," she writes, "my family hid God in the closet. We went to church twice a year and said grace before each meal but that was all. I personally didn't think there was a God, but sometimes when I looked in the mirror into the depths of my eyes I'd get scared and wonder, 'Who am I?' How was this solved? It took a serious family problem to shake us up and make us realize how wrong and strong willed we were. Thank goodness God did wake us up!"

What? "Thank goodness" for suffering? For a serious family problem, and the pain it caused? No. "Thank goodness" for the results that suffering worked.

And this is what the Christian asserts.[5] Not that he's glad for the suffering of anyone. And not that he shouldn't feel a responsibility to relieve human suffering. But the Christian looks at suffering—even the cases he can't begin to explain—and trusts God to work good through it. Somehow. "For examples of patience in suffering," says the Bible, "look at the Lord's prophets. We know how happy they are now because they stayed true to him then, even though they suffered greatly for it. Job is an example of a man who continued to trust the Lord in sorrow, and from his experiences we can see how the Lord's plan finally ended in good, and that the Lord is full of tenderness and mercy" (James 5:10-11).

And so there we are. We can't see the end. We can't *prove it,* either way. And so we're left with just one thing. Faith.

Faith vs. reason

At least, that's the way you usually see faith and reason. Contrasted. In opposition. It's as though we thought that one way of looking at reality is "reasonable" while the other is "a tenet of faith." And the hidden implication is that faith is *un*reasonable. That faith is, as the little girl said, believing something you know just isn't true.

But, as we've seen, this isn't the case. Faith and reason simply cannot be contrasted. Why? Let's think it through again.

At the beginning of this chapter we admitted that a conflict between a "scientific" and a "Christian" way of seeing reality does exist. The Bible presents a viewpoint of reality that is very, very different from the evolutionary picture.

We saw too that *any* such viewpoint is at best a *theory* —a way of interpreting and understanding facts. *It is not a fact itself.* And we suggested that a theory is *true* only when it fits the facts—when it is in full accord with and explains the reality, the data, it attempts to describe.

We then went on to note that, when it comes to the big

picture, no one has enough data to say with certainty that his theory of reality is true. No matter what tests we apply to the physical world, we cannot come up with *proof* that either the biblical or the evolutionary view of reality is accurate. Both sides in the controversy refer to facts, and then reason from them. But the reasoning, if we're honest, is just not conclusive.

This being the case, it's not accurate to say that the "Bible vs. Science" controversy is a controversy between faith and reason. It actually is a conflict of reason vs. reason, and of faith vs. faith!

Both sides can and do reason, and both sides ultimately rest their position on faith.

What do I mean by this? Simply that faith (what scientists might call presuppositions) underlies each position, *in exactly the same way!* The evolutionist presupposes (takes it on faith) that God does not exist, and that the world must and can be explained in purely natural terms. The believer presupposes (takes it on faith) that God does exist, and that the world can and must be explained in both natural and supernatural terms. Both sides bring their presuppositions to their study of the data. And, in the last analysis, it is *faith* (either evolutionary or theistic) that is exercised when a person takes sides.

This isn't to say that a person can't be *reasoned* into accepting either view. Of course he can. But it is to say that, when all the arguments are stripped away, and when a person is finally faced with the necessity of making a choice, that choice is made as an exercise of faith. It may be a "reasonable faith" (for all *that* phrase means is, "a faith for which reasons can be assigned"), but it is still a faith.

That's what is so interesting about one statement in the Bible. "By faith—by believing God—we know that the world and the stars—in fact all things—were made at God's command; and that they were made from nothing" (Heb. 11:3). That statement can be reversed. By faith—because we do not believe in God—we know that the world and the stars, in fact all things, were made by natural processes; and that there was no supernatural creation. In both cases the issue rests on faith.

Of course, the Bible supposes that its own viewpoint is far *more* reasonable than any other. "Since earliest times," it says, "men have seen the earth and sky and all God made, and have known of his existence and great eternal power. So they have no excuse for saying they don't know whether or not there is a God" (Rom. 1:20). You just can't look around you, see the order and intricacy of all things, and doubt that Someone planned and made them. Any more than you could look at the newest model car and seriously contend that it just "fell together" by "natural evolutionary processes" operating in inorganic matter. (And, of the two, things organic are far more intricately designed!)

But you still don't have to accept the biblical view. You may prefer to believe that the biblical picture of reality is not correct. And if you do, you can find reasons for your belief.

But there's one thing you can't do. You can't say that your view is *reasonable* and that the Christian view is "just a tenet of faith." You have to face the fact that your view rests on faith just as much as the Christian's. And that your assumption that "there is no God" is just as much a tenet of faith as is the Christian's assumption that "God is."

Does all this mean that in the end we can't ever know what's real? Can we ever know whether the Christian faith is anything more than a comforting way of looking at things—a psychological sop for moral and mental drop-outs?

No, it doesn't mean this at all. It only means that we're not going to find the evidence by examining the physical universe.

If we want to, we can take comfort by believing (with reason) that the biblical view *does* fit the physical facts, that it is true, in full harmony with reality.

If we want to, we can take comfort by believing (with reason) that the biblical view does *not* fit the physical facts. And we can use this discrepancy we think we find to reject God and to declare Him irrelevant. But this won't help us.

It won't change the pressures of the intangible within us. And it won't really answer the questions we must answer.

Steps to take

1. The author seems to doubt that the biblical view of reality can be proven or disproven from a study of the physical universe. Can you jot down the reasons he gives for this view? Check your memory against pages 59-75.

2. Do you have serious doubts about the reasonableness of the biblical position in the face of "scientific" objections? Why not check out some of the books suggested in footnote 4 of this chapter, and find out what reasons are given on the other side?

3. Why does the author say that the conflict between the biblical and evolutionary viewpoint is not one of faith vs. reason, but faith vs. faith and reason vs. reason? Do you agree or disagree? Why?

4. If you were faced, right now, with the necessity of
   making a choice between "God is" and "God is
   not," which would you choose?

6

Back to breakthrough

"Because I am a new Christian," writes a New Jersey fifteen-year-old, "I have many times doubted God's relevancy. Before becoming a Christian I felt I didn't need Him; but after finding out all about Him and His works, I know of His relevancy."

Interesting, isn't it? There's no talk here of the reasonableness of opting for God. No arguments from science or even from Scripture. Just the idea that "now I know."

In the last chapter we seemed to have just about given up on the tangible world. Apparently you can't prove anything by it, so why not just forget it?

But that's a wrong impression to give—or to get. Because Christianity claims to *work* in this world too—the world where we live. And the Bible, at least, claims that God does have control over events.

One of the biggest mistakes we make, one college friend suggests, is "to relegate God to an altogether different realm—the so-called 'spiritual' realm." Too often, another adds, we think that "God is necessary for eternity, but cannot do anything here and now. If we could only know that God was really acting every day and not just making sure that everything comes out the way it's supposed to in the long run, God would seem a lot more necessary."

Now, some kids claim that God is acting every day and that they can see it. They talk about Christ in a personal way, as if He were really around and really doing things. Like this Ohio college freshman: "What young people need most to see is Jesus Christ as a *personal* God and Saviour. How many times Christ has worked in my high school locker room during track season! He healed my asthma in front of the whole track team one cold, damp practice. They (my buddies) saw the *physical* difference in a Christian life. They saw a mediocre half miler give his legs and lungs to Christ and cut his time from a 2:21 to a 2:04 in a two-year span."

"I know there is a God," agrees a Pennsylvania junior, "because I've seen Him work in my life. Of course I always knew verses to back up God, but the most important fact is my own experience. I could do nothing if God didn't help me."

Now, it's true that it would be hard to *prove* that God ought to get the credit. Someone could say it's all "psychological." That wouldn't convince the kids who experienced it.

How do we resolve the issue? It almost seems there's an impenetrable wall between the tangible and the intangible. We can say that the intangible, or God, controls the tangible. Or we can deny it. But no one seems able to get around that barrier that keeps us from putting the two together. From really seeing the lines of cause and purpose that Christians claim run from all events and experiences in our world and in our lives right back to a sovereign and a loving God.

That's why we have to go back to breakthrough. But to a different kind of breakthrough. A very personal, very experiential, kind.

The kind of breakthrough we looked at before was breakthrough from the intangible world into the tangible. From God, to us. This took two forms, and both were historic. They happened in time and in space—in real history. The intangible took solid form in our tangible world.

One aspect of this breakthrough is Christ. And the Bible says some straight-out things about Him. "Christ is the exact likeness of the unseen God" is one. We couldn't *see* God, so God took a form we *could* see, and became a Man. The Bible goes on to say that God did not create this Son of His, "for he existed before God made anything at all" (Col. 1:15). And in another place it says that "God's Son shines out with God's glory and all that God's Son is and does marks him as God. He regulates the universe [the tangible world] by the mighty power of his command" (Heb. 1:3). So, the Christian believes, if you want to find out about the unseen God, take a look at His historic breakthrough. Look at Christ, and you'll meet God.

And we have the Bible. The Book that claims to tell it like it is—to show the way things *really* work in our own personalities and in the world around us.

This breakthrough, too, is a tangible one, and because we have it with us it can be examined. Even with all the rumors around about its supposed inaccuracy, every new bit of historical and archaeological evidence discovered serves only to confirm that it can be trusted. And a study of prophecy pretty well proves that it actually is of supernatural origin.[1]

But the Bible is important to us, not just as a Book from God, but because it shows us the way to make that other kind of breakthrough I mentioned. God broke through the barrier to us in Christ and in the Scripture. *But He did it so we could break through the barrier to Him.*

The peculiar thing about "faith"

Yes, that's right. It is at this point, thinking of breakthrough from our side, that Christians start talking about "faith." "We just take God on faith," they say. And this isn't particularly satisfying! At least, not until we understand a peculiar thing about faith—that the word doesn't mean what we usually think it does.

Go back a second to the contrast we talked about last chapter. The contrast, not of faith vs. reason, but of faith vs. faith and reason vs. reason. There I suggested that, whether a person opts for God or against God, his choice is basically an act of faith. He may assign reasons for believing in God, or reasons for not believing in God. But ultimately his choice just has to rest on faith. The evidence in the tangible world is such that one just cannot *know.*

Now, let's suppose that at the end of the last chapter you read Steps-to-take question 4, and decided that, right now, if faced with a choice, you would swing to the position "God is."

Does this mean that you "have faith"?

Not at all.

Let's say that you believe the weight of evidence is ninety-nine percent for the likelihood that God is. And you even go so far as to argue with friends for this belief. You're even on God's side!

Does this mean that you have faith?

Not at all.

Well, let's go further. Let's suppose that the evidence seems to you so conclusive that you are absolutely convinced and would say, "I *know* that God exists."

This is the position Gene took. He wrote, "Because of the evidences of Himself which He has shown to me as well as to all mankind (creation, nature, man's realization that sin is wrong—whether he admits it or not, etc.) God is something that *must* be reckoned with and sought after. God is Someone who is found and made relevant through the Scripture which He personally has given man in order that man might find Him."

Gene's convinced. Does this mean that Gene "has faith"?

Not necessarily.

For Gene adds, "God desires that man find Him. However, what is keeping me from finding Him? What must I do before I find Him?"

Somehow, while Gene believes that *God is*, his faith hasn't meant a breakthrough for him. Gene's still looking. He wants God. And he believes that God wants him. But he doesn't know how to find Him.

That's the trouble with this kind of faith. "Are there still some among you who hold that only 'believing' is enough?" asks the New Testament Book of James. "Believing in one God? Well, remember that the demons believe this too—so strongly that they tremble in terror!" (2:19).

Believing something about God and "believing" in the breakthrough sense are two very different things.

Some time ago I read a science fiction story about a spaceship crew that was captured by aliens and placed in a peculiar prison. It was made of metal as hard and solid as steel, and had no doors or windows. Yet every day the crew was fed as trays of food were thrust through that

solid metal wall. There were no openings or sliding panels. The food just went right through.

After a lot of dialogue, the crew decided that the prison was a test by the aliens to discover how intelligent humans are. After more dialogue, the ship psychologist hit on the solution. The walls weren't real at all! There was no metal; it was all illusion. They only appeared solid.

They all agreed that the psychologist's solution must be right. Yet, when some of the men went over and pounded on the wall, it rang as clearly as before. They pushed, and felt the metal press into their flesh. They closed their eyes and walked toward the wall—and smashed their noses.

They believed, but the wall was still there.

And then the psychologist got up and, with his eyes wide open, walked through the wall.

All the men believed, but only *one* had faith.

This is why I haven't tried to bring out all sorts of evidence in this book for things like the flood, or against evolution, or to prove that the Bible is God's Word, or anything like that. You could be convinced by the arguments, and come to believe as Gene believes. But even then you wouldn't have "faith." And you wouldn't have achieved breakthrough.

But breakthrough is the thing we've got to focus on. Why? *Because we only really know that God is, and find that He is necessary, when breakthrough has happened–for us.*

So we have to understand this thing about faith. Faith is really something *beyond* belief. It's another step. And a step of a different kind.

The one kind of faith is really conviction. You're intellectually persuaded. The other is a faith of commitment. That takes conviction, *plus* decision.

You've probably heard the story of the lady and the tiger. A young huntsman falls in love with a princess and is thrown unarmed into an arena, to stand facing two doors. He's told that behind one door is the lady, and behind the other door is a tiger, waiting to tear him to pieces. To complicate things he sees another lady of the court, with whom he had been in love, point toward one of the doors. The dilemma is this: did his spurned lover point to her rival or the tiger? And the story ends as the young man, reaching out to open one of these doors, stakes his very life on his choice.

Faith is a lot like this. All of us stand outside two doors. One is the door to a world of reality, the other to a world of illusion. There, to one side, is the Bible—a Book that claims to be God's Word to us—pointing out the right door.

We can *believe* as we stand there. But to *have faith* means opening the door and going through. We have to stake our lives on the belief that behind the door we'll find God.

The hard way

At this point someone always interrupts and complains, "But that's too easy! Only believe, and suddenly you're through? Suddenly you've got an inside track with God, and a ticket to heaven? Man, that's just *too* easy."

Actually, they've got it turned around. It's too hard!

Dee, an eighteen-year-old Texan, talks about her breakthrough and about her friends. "I am convinced that God is very relevant. Sure, I could *survive* without Him, but it isn't a question of surviving—it's a question of living. And turning my life over to God doesn't mean that I am chained and shackled by His will. The freedom that He gives me—to be myself—is fantastic.

"Many of my friends are searching and just stumbling around. They say that they envy me for believing and that they would like to believe in God too, but they just can't. Only, in reality, it isn't that they don't believe God is there; they just can't believe He cares and honestly will help them."

Believing *easy*? Never!

Well, why do so many people find this Christian kind of faith hard? Why, even when "they would like to believe in God," do they find they "can't"?

There are several reasons. One of them is that the conviction kind of faith and the commitment kind of faith are so different, and come from such different sources.

C. S. Lewis has an interesting story that points up what

I mean. He tells about a visit to surgery, and how it affects him. "My reason," he says, "is perfectly convinced by good evidence that anaesthetics do not smother me and that properly trained surgeons do not start operating until I am unconscious. But that does not alter the fact that when they have me down on the table and clap their horrible mask over my face, a mere childish panic begins inside me. I start thinking that I am going to choke, and I am afraid they will start cutting me up before I am properly under."[2] Lewis is convinced intellectually, but when he's put on the spot he finds that something else, welling up inside him, keeps him from trust.

This is the way it is with the commitment kind of faith in God. We may be perfectly convinced by good evidence that God is and even that He loves us, but something else—welling up inside—keeps us from trust.

Why is commitment faith so hard? Because its source isn't reason alone. It's related to our total personality— mind, emotions, will. And mostly because, as the morality gap we talked of in chapters 2 and 3 illustrates, there's something radically wrong with this total personality we have!

This is easy to demonstrate. How? Well, ask yourself a few questions. Why do we turn "God" into those bogeymen we met in chapter 4? Why do we have such irrational fears of Him—the real God—that well up in us as the fear of anesthesia welled up in Mr. Lewis? Why do we respond to God as we do?

The Apostle Paul talks about this in an important passage in Romans 1. "The truth about God is known to them instinctively; God has put this knowledge in their hearts" (v. 19). "Yes, they knew about him all right, but they wouldn't admit it or worship him or even thank him for all his daily care. And after a while they began to think up silly ideas of what God was like and what he wanted them to do. The result was that their foolish minds became dark and confused. Claiming themselves to be wise without God, they became utter fools instead" (vv. 21-22).

But *why?* Why, when truth about God is known, don't they worship Him or thank Him? Why do they do just the opposite?

This is an important point. Sometimes we think that people are "lost" because they don't believe in God. This passage suggests that we've got this idea turned around too. Instead, people don't believe in God because they're lost! Because something really is warped and twisted about their very natures.

Look at it this way. Ever seen a fellow and his girl walking down the street together? Soon their fingers brush against each other. What happens? Pretty soon they're holding hands! Somehow the hand of the guy and the hand of the girl had a natural affinity for each other.

Now, put the same girl at home ironing. Her fingers brush up against the hot iron. What happens? Wow! Does she jerk them away fast! The why is obvious. Fingers on a hot iron hurt. And she reacts instinctively to get them out of there.

Well, that's the Bible's point. If there were a natural affinity between people and God, we'd all be drawn *to* Him. Instead, our instinctive reaction is to pull away. To misunderstand Him. To throw up a false god whom we can feel comfortable rejecting, to cover up our knowledge of the real God of love who would make us face ourselves and realize that a real warp, a disfiguring scar, exists in our hearts and not in His.

So that's why. It's not that we're lost because we don't believe, but that we don't believe—in a commitment way—because we're lost and we really are sinners.

Now, I'm sorry about that word *sinners.* Not because I think we have to apologize for it, but because it's so misunderstood. As soon as it comes up we start thinking about the last thing we got caught for—or should have. But saying "sinner" isn't saying anything about the last thing we *did.* It's saying something about what we *are.*

Did you ever read passages like this in the Bible? "For people will love only themselves and their money; they will be proud and boastful, sneering at God, disobedient to their parents, ungrateful to them, and thoroughly bad. They will be hardhearted and never give in to others; they will be constant liars and troublemakers and will think nothing of immorality. They will be rough and cruel, and sneer at those who try to be good. They will betray their friends; they will be hotheaded, puffed up with pride, and prefer good times to worshiping God. They will go to church, yes, but they won't really believe anything they hear. Keep far away from people like that" (2 Tim. 3:2-5). Or take this bit about bitterness and selfishness: "Jealousy and selfishness are not God's kind of wisdom. Such things are earthly, unspiritual, inspired by the devil. For wherever there is jealousy or selfish ambition, there will be disorder and every other kind of evil" (James 3:15-16).

Now, these passages aren't talking about the things we *do.* They spotlight what we're like inside. And that's what the word *sinner* does. It spotlights what's inside. It spotlights what we called the "morality gap" a while ago, and it spotlights all such feelings and passions and swelling urges that each of us knows are inside. I know they're inside me. And you know they're inside you.

This is why "believing" is the hard way.

We may be "perfectly convinced by good evidence" as

we come up to the breakthrough point, but sin begins to twist and turn inside us, and something like a "mere childish panic" begins. We twist away from God and away from reality, and we fight Him—fiercely, blindly, desperately. And we find that we simply cannot break through.

It's a good thing.

Because only when we give up do we have the slightest chance.

Try

Try to find out. That's why I suggested earlier that you "try out" the morality gap. To see if you could make it on your own. And that's why I suggest now that you *try* to believe. To discover that twisting, elemental "you" that shrinks away from God no matter how you struggle to believe in Him.

When you've found out, you'll know why *both* breakthroughs are pictured by the Bible as absolutely necessary. We have to break through because, until we do, we're what the Bible calls "dead in sins" and "spiritually dead and doomed by . . . sins." What this means is that what we experience when we *try* to trust God or *try* to do right is our real condition. We're cut off—cut off from knowing God right now, and possibly cut off from Him forever.

But, again, this isn't something you have to take my word for. You can experience it.

Now, the other breakthrough—that of Christ *into* our world—was also necessary. He had to break through so that we could.

Probably you know the whole story as well or better than I. How "He died for our sins just as God our Father planned, rescued us from this evil world in which we live" (Gal. 1:4). And that "though you once were far away from God, now you have been brought very near to him because of what Jesus Christ has done for you with his blood" (Eph. 2:13). And that "when the time came for the kindness and love of God our Savior to appear, then he saved us—not because we were good enough to be saved, but because of his kindness and pity—by washing away our sins" (Titus 3:4-5). This, as the passage concludes, "all because of what Jesus Christ our Savior did" (v. 6).

Now, this isn't something I am going to try to explain. I'm not at all sure I can. Just how does Christ's death bring us to God? How does it change us inside and wash away our sins? I don't really know. But the Bible says that it does. And this, too, isn't something you have to take my word for. You can experience it.

But this is something we experience only when we stop trying. When we've discovered that the morality gap is there, and when we've tried and tried to pump up our "faith" and found that we can't. Then, when we turn to God and say, "God, You've got to do it," we find that *He* can.

This is really all that Gene needs. Remember him? He's the one who believed so strongly about God, but cried out at the end, "What must I do to find Him?"

The only answer I know is, nothing. You can't *do* anything at all. If the Bible is true, and God is really there like it says, then Christ has already taken care of all the doing. The only part I've got in the whole thing is to try—and, in trying, discover who and what I really am—a sinner. Then, because the "salvation that comes from trusting Christ—which is what we preach—is already within easy reach of each of us" (Rom. 10:8), all I *can* do is take it. Accept it. As the Bible says, "Anyone who calls upon the name of the Lord will be saved" (Rom. 10:13).

And salvation is what we're talking about. It's break-through. It's stepping into a new world—a world in which you can prove by experience that God is real and that God is relevant.

What is breakthrough?

It's hard to explain breakthrough. But perhaps it can be described by a Christian fellow who writes that "Christianity is a mere religion to many kids. How kids need to know that Christ is Christianity, and that this is a completely new way of life. They need to know the new dimensions they can experience in Christ."

Those aren't bad ways of saying it. A "completely new way of life." And, "new dimensions."

Lots of my correspondents thought of their experience as Christians in these ways: "God is necessary," says an Indiana girl, "so that I can love other people. Life is people, but I find I have no real concern or care for anyone else except through Christ." And a New Jersey guy shares exactly the same thing: "I am, or was, basically incapable of really caring about other people and their needs, without God supernaturally putting that love within me. This attitude change came only from a complete committal of my goals and lifestyle to Him."

Here's what a college girl says: "He holds the pieces together. Without Him there would be no rhyme or reason to life, and I probably would have committed suicide a long time ago. I've tried going it without Him and it just doesn't work. I've experienced a joy and peace in knowing Jesus: so much that He has become vital to my existence. If, after having known Him and experiencing Him, I were to turn away from Him now, I'd never make it. I'd never be happy; I'd never be satisfied."

According to all these descriptions, salvation (which is

what the Bible calls this particular breakthrough) hit them
inside. It changed them. "When someone becomes a
Christian," the Bible says, "he becomes a brand new person inside. He is not the same anymore. A new life has
begun!" (2 Cor. 5:17). So it's not that the world around us
changes. If we had a big nose before breakthrough, we're
sure to have one afterward. If we have a tough homelife,
with parents who fight or who are divorced, this won't
necessarily be changed. But *we* change. Inside.

Where we were empty before, now we're filled and
satisfied. Where we couldn't make it on our own, now we
find that we can do what we know is right, and we can be
what we should be.

How come? What's happened inside? Now, the Bible
says, "God is at work within you, helping you want to
obey him, and then helping you do what he wants" (Phil.
2:13). Note that. At work *in* you. Because "in you" is the
secret of the salvation the Bible describes. "For he has
kept this secret for centuries," it says in Colossians, "but
now at last it has pleased him to tell it to those who love
him and live for him, and the riches and glory of his plan
are for you Gentiles too, and this is the secret: *that Christ
in your hearts is your only hope of glory*" (1:26-27).

That's what it says. That when we turn to God for that
commitment-level faith, He steps into our lives Himself.
He's really here. So really here that we don't have to ask,
Is God there? anymore. We experience Him.

If, as the Bible says, and as our experience suggests, the
life we have is a warped one; if the nature we were born
with is a sinful one; if the personality we have developed
over the years is a disfigured one—why, then we need a
new life. A new nature, a new character. And according to
the Bible this is just what God says He does. Gives us a
new one. His own.

"I," writes the Apostle Paul, "have been crucified with Christ: and I myself no longer live, but Christ lives in me. And the real life I now have within this body is a result of my trusting in the Son of God, Who loved me and gave himself for me" (Gal. 2:20).

And when you've got that kind of life, you don't have to wonder or doubt anymore.

Steps to take

1. Take a quick check on yourself. If it's been *you* out of focus all this time, and not God, maybe you've been trying to operate on conviction faith rather than commitment faith. Are you clear on the difference between the two (pp. 80-84)?

2. Why does the author make so much over a "trying" kind of faith? How would you know when you've stopped trying?

3. If you want to dig in and question faith some more, try these passages of Scripture: Romans 4; Hebrews 11; James 2.

4. Do you think Christ, the real Person, lives in you? Why, or why not?

7

Who's boss?

"Just a minute! *Tell it like it is, buddy.* It's not all that simple."

Maybe these are your thoughts as you finish chapter 6. Just invite Christ into your life, and everything is solved? Life goes all beautiful, and God becomes real and necessary? Is that what's supposed to happen?

Not necessarily. With Christ, you've got the key to reality. You can open the door to a whole new world of experience. But it is new; a world to live in and explore. You didn't burst into the physical world full grown. You came in as a baby with a lot to learn. It's the same in this new world of living with Christ.

And one of the first things everyone has to learn is who's boss.

"I knew a born-again Christian at camp this summer," says Linda, an Ohio coed. "He was really mixed up. He felt God was no longer important in his life. He had prayed about God's will in his life, but He couldn't see God working, and everything was going wrong. He tried

to get close to God again, but he couldn't seem to. He was
utterly miserable and he became more self-centered each
day. I, as an outsider, could see God working in his life,
trying to break him. One night he and his roommate had
a good talk. This was in answer to many, many earnest
prayers by his roommate and me. The next day and for the
weeks after, he was completely changed. His face simply
radiated like I've never seen before. He could see God
working in every little thing, and it was beautiful to see
how completely he had surrendered his life to God."

In the first five chapters we've stood outside Christianity and looked at some of its claims without taking any
stand ourselves. Last chapter we saw that the only way
you can prove whether God is, and if He's necessary to
you, is to take a stand. You have to experience breakthrough yourself. This means trusting Christ to do what
He says He will—take on your sin and your sins, and give
you His own life. The cross and the resurrection tell us
that He can. We just believe His Word that He will.

But when we do this we're no longer outsiders. We're
on the inside. The inside of the biggest thing in the
world; a new life in which we can see and experience *both*
the tangible and intangible worlds. And experience great
things in each!

Now, note that I said, *can*. It isn't quite automatic. And
that's why the book didn't end with chapter 6. Breakthrough is the beginning; not the end. This is why our
viewpoint too has to change from now on. Instead of
looking at things as outsiders, we're going to start looking
at the Christian life as *insiders*. In a way, we'll try to see
how to toddle along in this new world and grow up in it.
Grow up until that exciting, real life with God that the
Bible calls "abundant life" is something we really experience. Some fellows and girls find it right away. Others get

off the track and find things are pretty miserable.

That's why we had to meet the guy Linda describes for us—to avoid that phony "it's all rosy" picture of life after breakthrough. For him, even though he had Christ in his life, he was still "utterly miserable" and "more self-centered every day." Both those big needs for God we talked about earlier, for satisfaction and for victory over ourselves, weren't being met. At all.

Now, he's not the only Christian with this problem.

Probably you were a Christian when you started reading this book. And maybe one reason you picked it up was that you'd been wondering too. How come, if you really know God as Savior, you're not satisfied and not able to do or to be what you really want to be?

Lots of guys and girls, brought up in solid Christian homes, feel just that way.

Let's look at how some of them described their Christian lives, and see if this is the way you may feel.

Jack, 18

"My reading of the Bible is very infrequent. I can't really understand it when I do read. I read a modern translation once in a while though. Most people would describe my witness as poor, but there are a few who would say it was pretty good.

"The hardest part of my Christian life is telling everyone what has happened to me. Living like Christ would want me to is pretty tough too. I need more determination. I always say, 'Well, I'll tell 'em when I'm older.' I also would need more Christianity of the kind that kids look up to.

"My spiritual life isn't very healthy. I go to church on Sunday; I listen, but I never apply what the pastor says to my life. I read the Bible once in a while and I pray when I need help—and I don't think this is right. I don't really know the Lord very well."

Sandy, 17

"I pray through the day for forgiveness and help but, as for giving thanks and praying for others at night, I'm always too tired and don't get up early enough in the morning. My Bible reading is pretty irregular, although I am on a Bible quiz team. I usually read to learn facts pretty much. As for personal devotions and meditation, I am pretty weak.

"My Christian witness isn't too hot. I do want to witness for Christ, but often I get involved in having fun and forget about witnessing. Also, as far as speaking for Christ, I haven't done much at all.

"I would like to be the kind of Christian that exemplifies Christ, always does His will, is consistent, and has real victory in his life over sin. But the hardest part is putting Christ first and allowing Him to always have control over every part of my life. I know I need more Bible meditation and prayer. Too, I must forget myself and make Christ the center of my life.

"I do want to do and find Christ's total will for my life. Yet I often find myself telling Christ one thing and doing another. Christ is my personal Savior yet I often have trouble keeping Him in charge (including with boys and clothes). Temper is another of my problems. Yet I know that if I allow Christ to be first, He will help me."

Phil, 16

"My spiritual life consists of explosions and silence. It is hot and cold. I no longer feel confident that I can promise the Lord something in a time of emotion. I have broken too many promises to Him. My emotions are almost uncontrollable at times. I feel sometimes as if my life is worthless. Sometimes I feel as though the only difference between life and death is my lungs moving in and out."

Marge, 17

"My Christian witness could be described as a big nothing. Verbally, I'm a total loss. My actions are my only credit—the way I live and speak, I hope, shows my Christianity.

"I pray daily—often during the day, too, because I find I'm always confronted by some kind of insurmountable problem. I would like to be the kind of Christian that Christ expects me to be. I would like to witness more and be able to conquer my doubts concerning the fundamentals in my life, like prayer and God's will.

"The hardest part for me is realizing that the Person I say my prayers to is really listening to my pleas. And witnessing—I need more knowledge and more willpower to conquer this.

"I feel my spiritual life is nothing to brag about. It is the closest you can get without being a non-Christian. Until recently I followed the theory that all you have to do to be saved is to believe in Christ. Now I realize that this isn't all there is to being a Christian. I am trying to be a better Christian, but it is a long, hard journey. Thanks for listening and letting me get it off my chest. Pray that I may better my Christian life."

Somehow these kids all sound a lot like Linda's friend. When they sit down to examine what, really, Christianity is and what it means in their life, they don't find a lot to excite them. They feel they ought to be more than they are. That they're missing something. That they're failures.

Now, how do you turn that around and become a radiating guy or girl who can "see God working in every little thing"?

Because He is. And life *is* rosy and exciting, when we can see it.

He gave in

Linda's analysis of the change in her friend's life is helpful when we're faced with a blah-type Christianity. "It was beautiful to see how completely he had surrendered his life to God." And, Linda continues by asking, "How did it happen? He had been resting on the cart with the burden still on his back. He wanted God to run his life, but he had his own idea of what that life was going to be. He learned that night to put his burden also on the cart and let it ride along too. He gave his life completely to God's keeping, and his whole outlook changed."

This idea of giving your life over to God is one many kids wrote of. "In my senior year in high school," one girl wrote, "I asked God to control my life. I had been a Christian for some time, but since then I have really felt the effects of His working in my life." "For me," says an Indiana fellow, "life without God proved quite pointless and absurd. I eventually began to realize that making God the center of my daily affairs was absolutely essential to a life with any real meaning." Another young man puts it even more strongly: "Obviously we must conclude that God only becomes significant when one gives Him *full* control."

Several who wrote me pinpointed the reason why this really *is* obvious. And they did it by viewing their experience in light of their personal relationship with Christ.

One was an Illinois eighteen-year-old, Dick. "I think the primary cause of lack of trust in Christianity is not having a real personal experience for yourself. It is very hard to believe the things said in the Bible and by other Christians if one's experience is not that of a close relationship with the Lord. Using the person I know best, I will use myself as an example of how it was before I really had a close relationship with the Lord.

"I was a junior in high school, and felt like Christianity was a bunch of empty promises. But finally I realized that if the Lord was great enough to create and then save us, He was of course great enough to know the wisest things for us to do with our lives, both on a long-term and day-to-day basis. When I *did* start living my life according to His will and direction, I could not believe the joy it caused me, and the way life was so much more meaningful and wonderful. Since that time, during the last two years, nearly every day has brought me a new awareness of the goodness and wisdom of God."

Now, why do we connect these two ideas: control and personal relationship? It's not hard to understand.

All of us have certain roles to play in all our relationships. For instance, the relationship between parents and children. This relationship lays certain responsibilities on both of us. Parents are to really love us, guide us (without being dictators), and help us along the path to mature adulthood. As their children we're to honor them and obey them. (This last may hurt, but we all know that's part of being a good son or daughter.)

Now, if either of us fails in his role at home and doesn't act as a good parent or good child, home becomes a very unhappy place. For harmony, for things to be in balance, we all have to live up to our own responsibilities—and we can't take the other person's part. You can't act like the boss at home and have things work out right.

Something like this takes place in almost all relationships. At school the teacher has one role; the student another. For school to mean something, each has to do his job in relation to the other. It's the same thing on the job.

The employee has his job to do, the employer his. You follow directions and give an honest day's work; he gives guidance you need and does a good job himself of running the business. When you're both doing your jobs, you'll both make money.

We meet a lot of people as equals, of course. But even our friends have times when they're in charge (like on a committee), or when we are. And for things to work out, there has to be the *right relationship* between the people involved.

That's why, when we think of personal relationship with God, we have to face the issue of *control.* Because in this relationship someone is always going to be in charge. It's going to be us, or Him. This is true even when we think of love as the key to our relationship. "Loving God," the Bible says, "means doing what he tells us to, and really that isn't hard at all. For every child of God can obey him, defeating sin and evil pleasure by trusting Christ to help him" (1 John 5:3-4).

This is very important, particularly when you tie a little phrase from the New Testament, "Stay always within the boundaries where God's love can reach and bless you" (Jude 21), with something Christ told His disciples.

One of them had asked the Lord how He would show Himself to believers after the resurrection. How could they really experience Christ—really "see" and know Him? Here's Christ's answer: I will only reveal myself to those who love me and obey me. And because he [who obeys me] loves me, my Father will love him; and I will too, and I will reveal myself to him" (John 14:23, 21*b*).

What it boils down to is this: Being a Christian only feels like the real thing—a vital relationship—when we realize that the other Person involved is God; and that that means *He's* got to be in charge. We can't act as if we're God. We have to let Him be God.

That was Laura's problem. She went on an Inter-Varsity retreat and decided to invite Christ into her life. The reason? Laura was too fat and had no boyfriends. The speaker promised that Christ would solve all her problems, so she made a bargain with God. "Come on in—and help me lose weight and get a boyfriend." But Laura didn't lose weight. And she didn't get a boyfriend. So she threw it all over as a bad joke.

Laura hadn't understood *who* in the relationship was to be God—who was to be in charge. And she found that snapping her fingers and expecting God to peel off the pounds and produce a fellow on call, just didn't work.

It won't work for you, either. Not if you're interested in

God as a shortcut to whatever *you* want. In this relationship there's only one God. Only one Boss. And it's Him;
not us.

What happens when you keep your life out of His
hands and take off as though you were in control? Look at
this warning: "Cling tightly to your faith in Christ and
always keep your conscience clear, doing what you know
is right. For some people have disobeyed their con-
sciences and have deliberately done what they knew was
wrong. It isn't surprising that soon they lost their faith in
Christ after defying God like that" (1 Tim. 1:19).

See it? *God can't be real to you if you won't let Him be
God.* You'll soon lose all sense of reality. For how can you
experience a personal relationship with a Person if you
constantly deny Him the place in the relationship that
He's supposed to take?

It's sad. Like a Colorado teen says, "God is relevant and
necessary, but those who have never experienced the real
joy of a personal relationship don't know what they are
missing, and are satisfied with less."

When you break through to reality by asking Christ
into your life, you're on your way to real joy through that
relationship. You shouldn't be satisfied with less. And
less won't satisfy you. But you'll never get there unless
you settle one thing first: who is going to be boss? Which
of you is going to play God?

But

Right! Let's look at some of the *buts.* After all, the kind
of decision I've been talking about isn't one to make
lightly. It's not the kind of thing you can just say. It's
something you have to *mean,* and you prove you mean it
by putting your whole life on the line. Not just that nice
hazy life of "someday"—but the solid, concrete life of

today and tomorrow too. Before we sign up for that, we ought to ask a few hard questions and get some honest answers. Like these:

What will I be getting into? I mean, since God is good and does love us, will it be easy? Will things go smoothly? Will I avoid some of the tough times I experience now?

And the answer to all of these is no. Not necessarily. It may be worse.

After all, if you were in charge of your life, you might take the easy way out of things. (Haven't you found that you usually do that now?) But God isn't going to run your life that way. He's going to have you doing the right thing and the best thing, even when it isn't easy. It's always worked like this. "And even though Jesus was God's Son," the Bible points out, "He had to learn from experience what it was like to obey, when obeying meant suffering" (Heb. 5:8).

A lot of Christians have had it rough too. Even great ones like the Apostle Paul. Think he was always on top of the world? Then read this: "To this very hour we have gone hungry and thirsty, without enough clothes to keep us warm. We have been kicked around without homes of our own. We have worked wearily with our hands to earn our living. We have blessed those who cursed us. We have been patient with those who injured us. We have replied quietly when evil things have been said about us. Yet right up to the present moment we are like dirt under foot, like garbage" (1 Cor. 4:11-13).

And this may be the kind of thing you're letting yourself in for. Maybe not, but it's a distinct possibility.

Now, Paul didn't see this as a drawback to being an all-out Christian. He even told us about his experiences, and how they felt. But he also told us about the other side of the experience. "I think you ought to know," Paul shared in another place, ". . . about the hard time we went through in Asia. We were really crushed, overwhelmed and feared we would never live through it. We felt we were doomed to die and saw how powerless we were to help ourselves; but that was good, for then we put everything into the hands of God, who alone can save us, for he can even raise the dead. And he did help us, and saved us from a terrible death; yes, and we expect him to do it again and again" (2 Cor. 1:8-11).

Even in the most awful situations, Paul was sure that God was with him, and knew he could "put everything into the hands of God." That's a real plus. Because if we decide to keep control, and try to dodge all the tough experiences of life, there's no guarantee we'll dodge successfully. And when we do get clobbered, if we've lost that living contact with God, the rough places *really* hurt.

Actually, when you turn yourself over to God you never know just what you're getting into, but you do know "how well he understands us and knows what is best for us at all times" (Eph. 1:8). God doesn't run our lives capriciously. He's always got purposes in view, and one of those that *always* operates is "what is best for us at all times."

I suppose it's often hard for us to believe that things that hurt us now are best in the long run. But that's the biblical view. And, like I said, the Bible does claim to picture things the way they really are. "When the way is rough," says the Book of James, "your patience has a chance to grow. So let it grow, and don't try to squirm out of your problems. For when your patience is finally in full bloom, then you will be ready for anything, strong in character, full and complete" (1:3-4). And in God's book, that's *good*.

So, if you turn your life over to Him, He'll run it for

your good. A lot of things He lets happen to you will probably hurt. You'll be glad later. If you can look beyond "right now." But don't expect a bed of roses.

What will I be giving up? This one bugs a lot of people. Like the one sophomore from Illinois says, "I think many kids are afraid of becoming true-all-the-time Christians, because they think they will not be as popular."

A true-all-the-time Christian has to be willing to give up *anything!* "The cause of my intense inner struggle," shares Ken, "was my concern over what my friends would think if I struck out as a Christian. My friends weren't Christians; I was popular, a member of football and basketball teams. My crowd were athletes and leaders in the school.

"To make matters worse, I was going steady with a girl who was not a Christian. We had been going steady for two years. My problem was not only what to do about her, but how my action, if I broke it off, would affect my standing in the group.

"Finally I came under such conviction that I yielded to God and became willing to let the chips fall where they would. I told my girl I was a Christian and no longer felt I could go to dances or the parties we used to attend. She didn't understand, but we kept going together until the summer after graduation from high school. She made a profession of faith, but seemed to grow very little. After a year in a Christian college, she dropped out, married a non-Christian, and to my knowledge doesn't attend church.

"Thinking back, I can see how strongly I was influenced by my peer group. It was their approval that kept me from Christ for some time. It is interesting that, in spite of my fears, my Christian stand at that time lost me no friends, and I remained in high standing with my school friends."

The thought of what it might cost him made this teen hesitate for a long time. In the end, he didn't lose anything. *But he might have!* And it might work out this way for you. It might really cost you.

But it's a choice you have to make. "Stop loving this evil world and all that it offers you, for when you love these things you show that you do not really love God" (1 John 2:15). That is what the Bible says. So face it. If God is going to be God in your life, what counts with Him has got to become what counts with you. It's like this passage says: "Don't copy the fashions and customs of this world, but be a new and different person with a fresh newness in all you do and think. Then you will see from your own experience that his ways will really satisfy you" (Rom. 12:2).

See the two things here? Don't buy the attitudes and values of the world around you. Look at things God's way. And then "from your own experience" you'll find His ways satisfy.

So that's it. What do you give up? Everything. Anything. Anything that doesn't fit in with God's way of looking at your life. And all you're sure of is that His ways "will really satisfy you."

What'll become of ME? That's another thing that bothers us sometimes. Am I giving up my own personality to become some sort of nameless slave of God's? Because all of us want to be somebody, don't we?

But how do we get to be somebody? Do we become *us* when we "do" something? "Oh yes, that's the guy who threw the pass that won the game in the Super Bowl." "Yes, that's the great evangelist. He won 10,000 souls last month!" Or, "Him? He did the first brain transplant!"

All these ways of finding ourselves, or of becoming our real selves, fail. Alvin Rogness talks about being somebody this way: "Status consists in being loved by someone. This is the secret. The psychologists and the juvenile courts agree that until or unless a person rests secure in the love of someone, he is in a bad way. He keeps on doing strange things in a fruitless search to be somebody."[1]

Finding yourself demands the freeing power of love—God's love. And that love is experienced when you're in right relationship with Him—under His control.

Does it work? Listen. "I feel a personal relationship with God is the only hope for a satisfied, creative, meaningful existence. God's unconditional love and acceptance of me is first liberating in my relationship with Him. Then I am able to love others. Many areas where I previously got hung up have been settled and fit into this concept of loving by faith."

Now, how does this New Jersey girl feel about herself? Has she lost her identity by turning herself over to God? No, she feels she found her real self—a self that's been freed by God to love Him, herself, and others.

"I often get the feeling," writes a Wheaton College student, "That I am trapped by my culture, trapped by the church, and trapped by myself. In the mass and flowing movement of millions of people, I am a number and a nobody. That is where God comes in. This is why God is needed and necessary. Christ told me, Eldon John Elseth, that I am a somebody. I am an individual and He, Christ, respects me on this basis.

"People do not like Christ. The church does not like Christ. This is because Christ is a Rebel. When everybody tried to squeeze Him into a mold, He wouldn't fit. When they thought they had Him figured out, He said the unexpected. Likewise, teenagers try to fit God into a mold. They put Him into a little box in the closet of their life.

"Do you see what I am driving at? Christ becomes necessary only if we let Him dominate our lives. When we try to dominate Him, He becomes unnecessary. God gives us this choice."

Want to try it? Try keeping God in a box in the closet of your life, and looking for yourself without Him. . .

But let Him dominate—let Him be God—and you'll find Him, and yourself.

What are my chances of making it? I mean, it sounds pretty tough. Like Sandy, don't we often tell the Lord one thing and do another? Maybe it's more honest to be like Phil, who said, "I no longer feel confident that I can promise the Lord something . . . I have broken too many promises to Him."

But that's exactly the point! *We can't make it.* That's why we *have* to give Christ full control. You see, putting "everything in the hands of God" means everything—even our trying.

That's what God asks. Total surrender. And that's just the decision we have to make.

A young Australian girl says something I like because it sort of sums up what we've been saying. "As a missionary's kid I have seen things I never dreamed possible. I saw God work, and man fail. I was almost sick at the hypocrisy of missionaries I met who used funds given in good faith and did very little work, had little concern, and showed little personal growth. But God has given me a desire to prove that I don't have to be like that. I don't have to be swallowed up. I will be broken to His will—and will have to be."

Steps to take

1. The author says that a lot of blah-type Christianity is caused by trying to play God. What does he mean?

2. Are you ready to say, with our Australian friend, "I don't have to be like that. I don't have to be swallowed up. I will be broken to His will—and will have to be"?
If you are, why not tell God so.
If you aren't, jot down the reasons. Do the thoughts on page 102ff. touch on any of your hang-ups?

3. What does this statement mean: *Christ never asks to share our lives, He invites us to share His.*

8

The great escape

"I'm rather confused about some matters," admits an eighteen-year-old from Indiana. "All I can say about things now is that our faith is not a code or set of moral standards, but a relationship with Christ. I've got that, and nobody can talk me out of it."

But what about codes and moral standards? To lots of people this is the center of Christianity. Anyone who begins a new life with Christ is going to stay concerned and confused and unhappy until he gets straightened out about codes and laws, and realizes that as far as he is concerned, relationship with Christ makes possible the great escape.

When I first read the descriptions of the Christian life given by the four teens quoted last chapter, I got the distinct impression that Christianity is a burden. Something that weighs us down; that crushes us with a sense of failure; that demands far more than we can ever do. It's almost as if someone asked us to climb Mount Everest without oxygen masks and, when we got halfway up, said, "OK. Now run the rest of the way!"

What gave me that impression? Things they said like
these: "The hardest part . . . ." "Living like Christ would
want me to is pretty tough." "I would like to . . . but the
hardest part is . . ." "I must . . ." "I often have trouble."
"I no longer feel confident I would be able." "I would like
to be able." "I am trying to
be a better Christian, but
it is a long, hard journey."

All these phrases point
up two things. These kids
have a strong sense of
ought and an equally
strong awareness of their
inability. And whenever
you put "I ought to"
alongside "I can't," you've
got frustration. Plain,
miserable, discouraging
frustration.

How do we break out of
this trap and find that
exciting life we're prom-
ised in Christ?

There are two pos-
sibilities we can see

at first glance *any* time "I ought" and "I can't" come together. One is to get rid of the "I ought." If your folks tell you, "Son, you ought to get A's in school," you're under pressure. Maybe you try, but just can't cut A's. It's frustrating unless you and your folks agree, "Son, I was wrong, You shouldn't get A's. You're a B student. You ought to get B's." *With the standard lowered within reach, there's no longer any need to be frustrated.* And that's one way to solve that kind of problem.

Another way to solve it would be to develop the ability to attain the higher standard. You can't get A's because you just haven't grasped the mathematical principles involved. Or because you haven't learned good study methods. Or because you missed a prerequisite course and lack the background. So you talk with the teacher, or get counseling on good study habits, or do some extra reading for the needed background. *If you develop your ability to the point where you can reach the original standard, there's no longer reason to be frustrated.*

The trouble is, neither of these ways out seems open to us. Does God drop His standards because we're in a new relationship with Him? Some people have said so. " 'You aren't saved by being good,' " Peter quotes them as saying, " 'so you might as well be bad. Do what you like, be free.' But" Peter advises, "these very teachers who offer this 'freedom' from law are themselves slaves to sin and destruction. For a man is a slave to whatever controls him" (2 Peter 2:19).

We can see this work out in ordinary life. Take the case of Renita, a girl who was sheltered until sixteen, and then turned loose from standards. Here's how a friend of hers tells it: "She was never allowed much freedom as a child. She never stayed overnight at a friend's house; her friends were all from her mother's circle of friends, and it was only in this group that she ever played with any girls her own age. Then, Renita went to high school. Technically she was growing up, but up to a certain time she was very deferential to her parents and they thought she was a very dutiful child. Then for her sixteenth birthday Renita's parents gave her a set of car keys and her freedom. Overnight Renita changed. She had the car constantly, and this gave her social status. Suddenly she was popular. She was spinning fast, always with a carload of friends just riding around. Her parents never knew her whereabouts and when they questioned or restricted her she could become the most hateful person I ever knew. She went on, not getting any better, until finally she went to our church college to be 'where the boys are.' I talked for a long time with Renita after her first year. She still hadn't changed much; only become more definite in thinking she knew best. She was very bitter, found life hard to impossible, hated 'religion,' and still blamed her parents for her mistakes. She has now quit school and is working in Texas. Independent? Yes. But not grownup."

Did release from standards make Renita happy? Or help her grow up? Or make her a better person? Not at all. And if God were to lower His standards for us, it wouldn't really help us either. That kind of freedom would only make us "slaves to sin and destruction," as the Bible says. So we shouldn't be surprised to read in the New Testament exhortations like "You already know how to please God in your daily living, for you know the commands we gave you from the Lord Jesus himself. Now we beg you—yes, we demand of you in the name of the Lord Jesus—that you live more and more closely to that ideal" (1 Thess. 4:1). And this: "Obey God because you are his children; don't slip back into your old ways—doing evil because you knew no better. But be holy now in all you do, as the Lord is holy, who invited you to be his child" (1 Peter 1:14-15).

Lower standards, for us? Hardly!

Then how about making us able to reach the standards? The New Testament doesn't hold out much hope here either. "The trouble," says Paul, "is not there [in the standard], but with *me*, because I am sold into slavery with Sin as my owner. I don't understand myself at all, for I really want to do what is right, but I can't. I do what I don't want to do—what I hate" (Rom. 7:14-15). And in saying this he sounds just like our four teens. Frustrated. Trying, struggling to reach the standard God sets, but always failing.

Isn't there any way out?

Surely. And it's one we'd never think of. What it boils down to is this: God removes *both* frustrating elements. He gets rid of standards as something we have to struggle to keep, and He gets rid of the "I can't" by showing us that *He* can.

A look at law

"I wish," one coed wrote me, "that Christ were more often presented as a Friend and Companion and the One who came to set us free from the law. I think freedom and joy in the Christian life are the hardest things for a non-Christian to believe in—simply because so many of us don't have them."

What does she mean, "set us free from the law"?

Often sincere Christians become upset when anyone talks about freedom from law. Looking back at Renita, you can see why. They realize that it's hard to handle complete freedom. Why, you might do *anything*! And surely that isn't right.

There were people like that in New Testament times.
And there were people, like Renita, who would misunderstand and misuse Christian freedom. "You are free
from the law," the Bible says to them, "but that doesn't
mean you are free to do wrong. Live as those who are free
to do only God's will at all times" (1 Peter 2:16).

Yet, over and over again, the Bible insists on one thing:
we *are* free from the law. The law, as a standard to live up
to, just doesn't apply to Christians.

To understand why, and to see why our coed friend is
so excited about the "freedom and joy" she's found when
the pressure is off, we have to note a few things about the
biblical concept of law. A look at any modern dictionary
shows how complicated the meaning of this simple word
can be. And the Bible has a few twists of its own. As well
as referring to rules governing behavior, "law" can refer
to the customs and worship practices of Old Testament
times; and "the Law" is sometimes a code word for the
first five books of the Old Testament. Sometimes people
make a distinction between the "moral law" (moral rights
and wrongs such as are outlined in the Ten Commandments) and the "ceremonial law" (special worship festi-
vals which the Jews were to attend, or their sacrificial
system). Often people who make this distinction say that
they are no longer under the ceremonial law (we don't
bring sacrifices) but that we are under the moral law (we
still have to do what's right). But this distinction isn't
much help when we're caught between the "I must" and
the "I can't" in daily experience! It's the right and wrong
that bother us!

Actually, the New Testament passage that talks of "the
old system that came to an end" refers to both kinds of
law. Even the moral law isn't supposed to apply to us
(2 Cor. 3:6, 11)! So we're right with the Bible when we say

that, in this chapter you're reading, "law" will mean *any standard set by God which men have been told they must obey.*

We really are going to get rid of that "I ought" because God has really gotten rid of it for us!

But how? Let's see.

By seeing law's purpose. When you look at the Bible this comes through perfectly clear. God didn't set up standards so that we would live up to them. "Why were the laws given?" asks the Bible. "They were added, after the promise was given, to show men how guilty they are" (Gal. 3:19). "The Ten Commandments were given," it says in another place, "so that all could see the extent of their failure to obey God's laws" (Rom. 5:20). And, "no one can ever find God's favor by being good enough. For the more we know of God's laws, the clearer it becomes that we aren't obeying them, for his laws serve only to make us see that we are sinners" (Rom. 3:20).

Some people get upset at this line of thought. They think God is unfair to set up laws and standards no one can keep. He would be if His purpose were to torment and frustrate us. But that's not His purpose. His purpose is always to make us see that we need Him.

It's like a person who is an alcoholic and won't admit it, even to himself. "I can stop anytime I try," he says. So, what can we do? We can't help him until he wants help. And he won't want help until he faces the fact that he can't go it alone. And how does he find that out? Just one way. *Try to stop.* Set up a standard, a test. And when he flunks it, he may realize that he has to turn to someone outside himself for help.

That's what God has done for us with the law. He's set up a test. Take it, and flunk. No matter who you are. If you try to live up to God's standards, you'll fail. And when you fail, you may realize you have to turn else-where, outside yourself, for help. You may realize that "the only way out is through faith in Jesus Christ" (Gal. 3:22).

This is why the Bible can say, "Laws are good when used as God intended. But they were not made for us, whom God has saved; they are for sinners who hate God, have rebellious hearts, curse and swear, attack their fathers and mothers, and murder. Yes, these laws are made to identify as sinners all who are immoral and impure (1 Tim. 1:8-10).

So if you've been frustrated trying to live up to Christian standards, and trying to do what the Bible says is right, don't be surprised. You're supposed to be frustrated if you try to keep them! "We aren't saved [delivered] from sin's grasp by knowing the commandments of God," the Bible says, "because we can't and don't keep them" (Rom. 8:3). So we really do have to be freed from law. God does have to get rid of the standards if we're going to find the freedom and joy offered in our new life, and if we're to get rid of failures and frustrations.

By seeing what else law says. Sometimes we concentrate so hard on trying to do what we think laws and standards tell us to do, we miss something else they say.

Now, certainly biblical standards and laws do tell us what's right. And the Bible does say to Christians, "I want you always to see clearly the difference between right and wrong, and to be inwardly clean, no one being able to criticize you from now until our Lord returns. May you always be doing the good, kind things that show you are a child of God" (Phil. 1:10-11).

But they tell us something far more important. (More important even than the message we looked at before—

that we can't keep them.) *They tell us what God is like.*

God's standards are an expression of His nature. "Be ye holy," says a passage we've already looked at, "for I am holy." In all standards God is saying both "be like Me," and "this is what I am like." That's why "good kind things" do go along with being a child of God. We're supposed to be like our heavenly Father—to bear the family resemblance.

"Now you can have real love for everyone," the Bible says to believers, "because your souls have been cleansed from selfishness and hatred when you trusted Christ to save you; so see to it that you really do love each other warmly, with all your hearts. For you have a new life. It was not passed on to you from your parents, for the life they gave you will fade away. This new one will last forever, for it comes from Christ" (1 Peter 1:22-23).

And in saying this, the whole issue is shifted from one of living up to standards, to one of living the new life. From laws, to personal relationship with God.

So what the law says to *us* isn't "Keep me." God really isn't interested in our serving Him "in the old way, mechanically obeying a set of rules, but in the new way, with all of your hearts and minds" (Rom. 7:6). The law does tell us about God; but as long as we look at it as a set of rules to obey, we're sure to miss Him. If we concentrate on the standards, we're sure to fall short of the goal of Christlikeness. If we concentrate on our relationship with God, and living that new life with Him, we'll finally find freedom—freedom to do and to be what we really want to be.

Let me say it again. In living in this new world, *we are to forget all about standards as rules to keep.* They simply do not apply to us. At all. And only when we forget about them as rules we ought to keep can we come close to being the kind of person they describe!

Now don't misunderstand what I'm saying here. The Bible does show us, very clearly, right and wrong. Saying that we're not to read biblical standards as rules isn't saying, in any way, that we're to forget about living a life that is in complete harmony with the Word of God. Not at all. Because the Bible really does show things the way they are; it tells it like it is. If God shows us a pattern of life in the Scriptures, and He does, this is the pattern of life He wants us to experience. This is the pattern of life that will prove exciting and real and abundant for us. It's just that the secret of actually living a life that fits the biblical pattern is not "Read the Bible as a rule book." It's "Avoid reading it as a rule book!"

Is that hard to understand? Then look at it like this. When a baseball coach introduces you to the game, he'll probably tell you the point of the game is to score. But when he sends you up to bat, what does he tell you to concentrate on? Home plate? Of course not. Sure, the point of the game is to get there, but a good coach knows that you've got to keep your eyes on the ball. Because unless you hit that, you'll never score.

When God sends us up to bat in our new life with Him, He does just what the coach does. He may say that, sure, the object of the game is to score—to be and to act like Me. But He also coaches you on *how to win*. And His first advice is Get your eyes off home plate! Don't look at the standards that tell *where* you're supposed to arrive. Fix your eyes on the ball and concentrate on the *how*. It's only when you hit the ball that you'll get to first base.

Eyes on the ball

Let's say that we buy this so far. We're not going to pay any attention to the standards. For us, they don't exist.

We just plan to concentrate on the ball, believing that if we hit it we'll score with right and wrong. Fine. But, what is "that ball"? Can't we just believe that God will help us keep the standards, and try with His help? Is that the ball?

No, the Bible points us to something very different. Here are some passages that hint at it: "You are living a brand new kind of life that is continually learning more and more of what is right, and trying to be more and more like Christ who created this new life within you. In this new life one's nationality or race or education or social position is unimportant; such things mean nothing; whether a person has Christ is what matters, and he is equally available to all" (Col. 3:10-11). And this: "Out of his glorious, unlimited resources he will give you the mighty inner strengthening of his Holy Spirit. And I pray that Christ will be more and more at home in your hearts, living within you as you trust in him. May your roots go down deep into the soil of God's marvelous love; and may you be able to feel and understand, as all God's children should, how long, how wide, how deep, and how high his love really is; and to experience this love for yourselves, though it is so great that you will never see the end of it, or fully know or understand it. And so at last you will be filled up with God himself" (Eph. 3:16-19). Here's just one more: "Each time He [God] said, 'No. But I am with you; that is all you need. My power shows up best in weak people.' Now I am glad to boast about how weak I am; I am glad to be a living demonstration of Christ's power, instead of showing off my own power and abilities" (2 Cor. 12:9).

See the key thought running through each of these passages? Christ created this life within you—whether a person has Christ is what matters—He is available to all—Christ more and more at home in your hearts, living within you—at last you will be filled up with God Himself—I am with you; that is all you need. Each passage says something about our new life. *That somehow God Himself is now living within us.* That when we break through to Him by faith in Christ, He breaks through to us; He comes into our personalities and now *lives* within us.

This is a lot different from helping *us* keep His standards. From giving us a leg up when we've almost reached the top. The fact is that when we try to keep the standards, we fall horribly short. We don't even get close to the *bottom*, much less the top. So God couldn't just "help" us do it. He has to do it *for us*.

Why? Remember that "something else" we said standards in the Bible say to us? They tell us what God is like. Because standards flow out of His moral nature. You wouldn't, even if you had the authority, make a law that everyone has to kill and eat his mother when she reaches age fifty. That's against *your* moral principles, so you wouldn't make that law for someone else. The kind of laws you would make would depend on, and show, the kind of person you are.

It's the same with God's laws. And that's why they don't say, as rules do, "Keep us." What they really are saying is "Be like me." And this is what's so impossible. *The standard is God's own character, and He is the only One who can ever be that good!*

That's why God's solution to the frustration we feel when we try to keep His standards is never to increase our ability. Even He couldn't make us able to be like Him. So what does He do? He comes into our life Himself. And once He's here with us, He's able to live out His own life through us. Remember what Paul said? "I have been crucified with Christ: and I myself no longer live, *but*

Christ lives in me" (Gal. 2:20). That's it. Christ lives in us. And so He Himself is available to keep the standards He set, as He lives in and controls us.

The gap bridged

So the morality gap, that chasm between what we know is right and what we actually do, is finally bridged. It's bridged not by lowering the standards or by making us able to keep them, but by Christ filling our lives and living His life in and through us.

And, in this context, some of the things kids have been saying throughout this book begin to make sense. Remember some of them. Like the girl we met in chapter 1. She wrote, "In my sophomore year of college, I met some visiting guys on campus who *obviously* had some dimension to their lives I just did not have. They explained that it was a relationship with a Person, Jesus Christ, and proceeded to tell me how they quit trying to change their lives and please God, and asked Christ to change them. That was the beginning of an honestly new life for me—no more phoniness, hypocisy, or performance. Just a day-by-day, minute-by-minute walk of dependence upon Christ. It's really out of sight!"

And the Pennsylvanian we met on page 78. "I always knew verses to back up God, but the most important fact is my own experience. I could do nothing if God didn't help me." And Dee, the Texan: "Turning my life over to God doesn't mean that I am chained and shackled by His will. The freedom that He gives me—to be myself—is fantastic!" And this New Jersey guy: "I am, or was, basically incapable of really caring about other people and their needs, without God supernaturally putting that love within me. This attitude change came only from a complete committal of my goals and lifestyle to Him.

Can you see it? The "ball" we've got to fix our eyes on is
Christ Himself. And the issue—the only issue—is that of
our relationship with Him. (In the next chapter we'll see
the big role the Bible plays in this.) But how foolish it is to
try to bridge the gap by struggling to be a better
Christian. "Have you gone completely crazy?" the Bible
asks some men who tried to grow as Christians by keeping the standards. "For if trying to obey the . . . laws
never gave you spiritual life in the first place, why do you
think that trying to obey them now will make you
stronger Christians?" (Gal. 3:3).

That's a real good question. Breakthrough was made on
a principle of faith in which Christ did—not by struggling
to do something ourselves. Why should God change His
way of doing things once we've become believers? If we
were saved by faith in Christ, why shouldn't God plan to
go on delivering us daily from our sin and frustrations in
the same way by faith in Christ?

Do you suppose the Bible really means what it says?
That "you can never please God without faith, without
depending on him" (Heb. 11:6). Does *never* really mean
never? In daily life too?

I think so. And the Bible certainly says so: "And now
just as you trusted Christ to save you, trust him too for
each day's problems; live in vital union with him. Let
your roots grow into him and draw up nourishment from
him. See that you go on growing in the Lord, and become
strong and vigorous in the truth you were taught. Let
your lives overflow with joy and thanksgiving for all he
has done. Don't let others spoil your faith and joy with
their philosophies, their wrong and shallow answers built
on men's thoughts and ideas, instead of on what Christ
has said. For in Christ there is all of God in a human
body; *so you have everything when you have Christ,* and

you are filled with God through your union with Christ"
(Col. 2:6-10).

So go on. Get your eyes off the standards, and stop
trying. And get your eyes on Christ, and start depending
on Him.

In a moment

In a moment we'll go on to another chapter, and take a
look at this depending on Christ bit and at growing in
Him, just as the Bible says we must. But first, let's set
down just a few thoughts we should be clear on from this
chapter, and always remember.

1. The great escape is *from* the frustration of trying
and failing to live up to God's standards. It is an
escape *to* a real freedom and joy, found only in being
the kind of person God want us to be, and the kind of
person we really want to be too.

2. Freedom from standards and from law never
releases us to live immoral lives or to do things that
we know are wrong. "Don't be misled," the Bible
says, "remember that you can't ignore God and get
away with it: a man will always reap just the kind of
crop he sows! If he sows to please his own wrong
desires, he will be planting seeds of evil and he will
surely reap a harvest of spiritual decay and death
(Gal. 6:7-8).

The kind of misery Renita experienced always ac-
companies freedom that is misused this way. And
misery isn't what God offers us. He loves us far too
much.

3. Freedom doesn't mean escape from personal responsibility. It does mean freedom and full release
from the frustrations of a responsibility we can never
fulfill; a responsibility to try to be good, a struggle to

keep God's standards. The freedom God offers involves a new and simple responsibility in which our part is to keep turning over control to Christ. To daily let Him live His life through us.

Often our desires will pull us two ways. We'll want to do what we know is wrong, and we'll want to do what is right. "Who," says the Bible, "will free me from my slavery to this deadly lower nature? Thank God! It has been done through Jesus Christ our Lord. He has set me free" (Rom. 7:25). Our need is to turn to Him.

4. "Keeping our eyes on the ball" means staying close to Christ, developing our personal relationship with Him. "If we stay close to him," the Bible promises, "obedient to him, we won't be sinning either. The person who has been born into God's family does not make a practice of sinning because now God's life is in him, and so he can't keep on sinning, for this new life has been born into him and controls him—he has been born again (1 John 3:6*a*, 9). What we need to concentrate on, always, is developing our relationship with Christ. When Christ is in control, when we're in fellowship with Him, then He will live out his life through us, and we'll experience full freedom and full joy.

Maybe it all sounds too easy? Too "pat" a solution? In some ways it may be, but in other ways it's not. "Now I have given up everything else—" says the Apostle Paul, "I have found it to be the only way to really know Christ and experience the mighty power that brought him back to life again, and find out what it means to suffer and die with him. So that whatever it takes I will be one who lives in the fresh newness of life of those who are alive from the dead" (Phil. 3:10-11).

Whatever it takes.

That's not pat. And not easy. It demands decision. And it doesn't leave any other way out.

But it's worth it. It's really a *great* escape!

Steps to take

1. On page 120 the author says there is a difference between seeing God's standards as telling us *where* we're going, and as telling us *how* to get there. What's the difference, and why is it important?

2. Do you feel frustrated about anything you think you ought to do as a Christian, but which you think you can't? Jot it (or them) down.

3. How have you tried to lick the frustration? Did you try either solution suggested on pages 112-13? Did it work?

4. How is the solution suggested on pages 115-25 different from the one you tried? How would it work in each case?

5. How much does freedom to be and to do what you feel you ought to be and do mean to you?

9

Getting to know you

Judy, a New Jersey sophomore, has a problem. "Why does God keep us hanging on?" she asks. "I mean, there are so many things wrong that should be right; or complicated and should be simple. They say God's always with you and you just have to take their word for it. There isn't any proof to be offered."

Judy would like it to be much simpler. And to be the kind of thing you don't need to take someone else's word for—something you can experience yourself.

A friend of Judy's in New Jersey raises an issue that bugs lots of fellows and girls. *How* do I get to know God? "He has not, I believe, shown His love or understanding in my prayers and worship. I have no assurance through His actions that I am saved, because He doesn't answer my prayers. Not just in the way I wish, but not at all." This girl has tried communication both ways: she's prayed to God, and she's looked for God to answer. But as far as she can see, neither she nor He is getting through!

Yet, in developing any relationship, communication is

the key. How can two people get to know each other if they don't communicate? If they don't openly and honestly share their thoughts and their feelings with each other?

That seems particularly clear to twenty-two-year-old Virginia. "God must communicate with me to project His will, His thoughts and His 'answers' to prayer. How does He do it? If the Bible is the way, then the communication is too general to be specifically aimed at me. So it is impossible for me to have genuine fellowship, for that implies two-way communication. If He speaks through my mind and my own inclinations and feelings, then how can I really know that God is talking, and not just my own subjective wants and fears? If He speaks through circumstances, how again can I know it's Him and not simply chance and probability and naturally occurring events, with no God moving behind them? What is left other than actual voices, and appearances, etc.—and He doesn't appear to be in that type of business anymore."

Virginia has worked out a tentative solution; one she's not perfectly happy with, but one she's found she can live with. "I believe in a personal God interested in my life because of what God says in the Scripture. Therefore He is working in my circumstances and desires and inclinations because He loves me and wants the best for me. It all boils down to faith."

She's certainly hit the crucial problems squarely, and in her statement "it all boils down to faith" has come up with a basic principle. (Provided she means the same thing by "faith" that the Bible means.) But this isn't the complete answer. The complete answer should lead her to what one college fellow calls "the reality of Jesus Christ—how to make Him real and not just a good image, and how to make Christianity more than just a habit."

Somehow God has to be more than just an idea to us.
So let's take a look. How *do* we get to know God? How
do we experience the reality of Christ in us, the relationship that God says we have with Him?

Communication and response

Often we think of communication with God as Judy's
friend does. As something that begins with prayer and
ends with answered prayer. "He hasn't shown His love,"
she felt, "because He doesn't answer my prayers." What
she's really saying is this: I've tried to communicate, but
God just won't do His part. He won't respond to me.

Now, certainly God welcomes our prayers. The Bible
assures us of that. But even when it talks about prayer,
you get the clear impression that the pattern of communication isn't what Judy's friend seems to think. It is not
from us to God and back to us again.

For instance, take John 15:7. "If you stay in me and
obey my commands," Christ says, "you can ask any re-
quest you like, and it will be granted!" Note the pattern
here. God initiates the communication; we respond to
Him, *then* we're in the place where we can pray to Him
and have Him respond. It's just as we saw earlier. Remember Jesus' answer to His disciples when they asked
how He would show Himself experientially to them? "I
will only reveal myself to those who love me and obey
me" (John 14:23). The pattern has to start with God's
communication to us, and involve our response to Him.

This is a lot like Laura's misunderstanding (remember
her from chap. 7?). So often we all forget who is God in
this relationship we have with Christ. Yet we have to face
it. *He isn't on call for us.* And if we treat Him this way, if
we insist on expecting Him to communicate *our* way,
prayer is going to be an awfully empty monologue! The

lines we so often feel are down are going to stay down.

How then is communication established? What is God's pattern for communication? One that recognizes who He is and who we are, and that frees God to show Himself to us in a vital, exciting way. His pattern has three basic elements: the Bible, response and faith.

God speaks to us. Earlier I suggested that some people use the Bible wrongly. They look at it as a book of rules to be obeyed; as a book of standards they have to live up to. And so the Bible becomes to them what it seemed to Virginia—"too general to be specifically aimed at us."

But, however we take the Bible, the believer is not to see it as a list of rules and standards. Yes, the Bible does tell us what is right. But in doing this the Bible also shows us *God.* And God, in the Bible, speaks to us about Himself.

This is the first thing we have to understand if we're to find that the Bible is God's *personal* communication to us. Why? Because of the difference this understanding makes in how we approach the Bible, and in what the Bible comes to mean to us.

Look at it this way. Suppose a friend's mother is a nag. Every day when he comes home, she shouts at him, "Clean your room." "Hang up your clothes." "Don't go out until you finish your homework." "Clean your fingernails." "Remember, you're only allowed to be on the phone for ten minutes."

Or suppose all her talk is critical. "I don't know why you insist on wearing your hair like that. It looks awful." "Can't you do *anything* right?" "Why don't you get good grades like your sister?" And so on, and so on, and so on.

Now, is she communicating with him? Sure. But what's his response? That's pretty clear, isn't it? *Get me away from her!*

Well, how do *you* view the Bible? I'm afraid that to many of us, who have been hung up on the idea that it's a rule book, it's a lot like that mom. And we have the same basic attitude toward the Bible any normal kid would to his nagging mom. Man, keep me away from that!

But what if your mom, or anyone else you know, doesn't major on criticism and isn't a nag? What if she just sits down with you, listens to what you have to say, tells you (without criticism and without nagging) what she feels and how she thinks, and wants you to share with her? Then communication is meaningful. Then we want it. Because then communication helps us both grow.

That's the thing about the Bible. That's what reading it is supposed to be like—and can be like. We don't come to it to find out how wrong we are. (We usually know that.) We come to find out what God is like; to let Him share His thoughts, His feelings, His way of looking at life, His very personality—knowing that we can talk to Him in prayer and be just as open as He is. God *loves* us. We don't have to be phony with Him, and He won't be phony with us.

So that's one thing about the Bible. We can come to it expecting to learn about God, and expecting Him to share Himself with us. We can come to it knowing that we'll get the straight scoop. That what God says to us in the Bible is true—a sharp and clear picture of the way things really are and the way things have to be in our lives if life for us is to be abundant. And, most exciting, we can come for very personal guidance. For practical help with the problems we face in our daily grind.

How can a book that's general, for everyone, provide that kind of guidance? It's simple. *We've got the Author inside to tell how His Word relates specifically to each "me"!* That's what the Bible is pointing out when it says that "He lives within you, in your hearts, so that you don't need anyone to teach you what is right. For he teaches you all things, and he is the Truth, and no liar" (1 John 2:27). God can apply His general communication to each of us personally—and He will! That's what Donnie, from Illinois, discovered. "I started having my own devotions. They were spasmodic—not only as to gaps between days, but I'd read a verse here and then several someplace else. This didn't seem to be adding too much to my Christian life. So finally I attempted to read the New Testament through, a chapter a day. Before each chapter was read, I asked the Lord to show me something for that day from that particular chapter. Some days it seemed as though the whole chapter was intended just for me. Other days some verses or perhaps some phrase stuck out. But I've found that devotions can be meaningful! It never ceases to amaze me when I sit down and just praise the Lord for what He has done for me through Christ."

She's found, with others, that Christ really can make His general communication intimately personal. "I find," says another girl, "that as I ask God to bless the spiritual food He has for me in the Word, He does just that." And if we start our relationship with this communication *from* God—coming to the Word to meet Him and to find His guidance for us as individuals—He will speak to us there.

We respond to God. So far we've looked at God's pattern for opening communication with us. How do we respond? How do we "talk back"?

Our first thought might be "in prayer." And in a sense this is, of course, right. But if we go back a minute to an earlier thought, we'll see the answer is really something else. Remember this verse? "If you stay in Me and obey My commands, you may ask . . ." *Something comes before prayer.* And that something is staying close to Christ and obeying Him.

Now, again, we're not thinking here about a struggle to live up to any standard. We stay close to Christ when we let Him be God, and when, under His control, we let Him live out His life through us. You can see how this has to involve obedience. Not blind obedience to a rule, but a willingness to do what Christ directs.

Remember how we viewed the Bible in chapter 5—as an accurate portrayal of reality. The Bible tells it like it really is.

Picture yourself at an amusement park, walking through a house of mirrors. It's your first time through, and everywhere you look you see reflections of yourself. You look for a corridor, but all you see is reflection and illusion. But you have a friend with you who knows his way through. He's been in the house of mirrors before, and he's learned to look at the floor and follow the pathway worn by others' feet! If you trust him, he can lead you through. He can see the reality. You, looking at the mirrors, see only illusion.

That's a lot like life. Everywhere we look we see illusions that masquerade as reality. We have choices to make: what will we do when we graduate; how about dating; what about a job; about school; about popularity. Every day a myriad of choices present themselves, and we have to sift through them and decide. But how will we decide? What are the right, the best choices? Which will lead us through life on the right path?

With Christ in our lives, we have a Friend at our arm who can separate the reality from the illusion, who can guide us through. But to keep from banging our noses against life's illusions, we have to stay close to Him and obey Him. When He says "left," we have to turn left. And when He says "right," we have to go right. And we have to go straight ahead when He says "go" and wait when He says "stop."

You see the kind of obedience the Bible means? It's not a "club and law" type thing; not an impersonal lock step "we all do it *this* way." It's the direct, personal guidance of Jesus Christ as a real Person within us, who can and who will direct us as we remain responsive to Him.[1] And He speaks to us through His Word.

This is where our communication with God has to begin. With responsiveness to His biblical communication to us. And unless we're willing to begin here, we'll never get beyond that "you just have to take their word for it" stage. But when we do respond, we begin to experience the reality for ourselves.

We rely on God

Communication and response are something that seem, at first, to happen *inside* us. They have to do with our personal relationship with Christ: the Person who lives intangibly within us. But when we talk about relying on God, when we talk about *faith*, we're looking outside again. Outside ourselves and our personalities at the tangible world we all live in.

And here we begin to wonder. Maybe God can help me inside. Maybe God can work in my personality. But does God work in events, in the things that happen to me daily? It's Virginia's question all over again. "How can I know it's Him and not simply chance and probability and naturally occurring events, with no God moving behind them?"

In chapter 5 we saw that all of us take our presuppositions about the world on faith. Since I wrote that, I heard a science professor at Northwestern University, where I took some classes, state his faith: "The scientist has faith that God has not, will not, and cannot enter into the physical world"—that this is the kind of world we live in.

It seems obvious that God doesn't make a habit of working outside the framework of natural causes and events. The Bible only records four periods of real miracles: in the time of Moses, the time of Elijah and Elisha, the ministry of Christ, and the ministry of the early apostles. Yet the Bible makes it clear that even when God isn't performing miracles, God is controlling history and the lives of individuals. His control is exercised *through* the "natural" events. God can act just as easily in the natural course of things as when He chooses to interrupt the natural course of things.

Now, just as the scientist I quoted has faith that God

isn't intervening in our tangible world, *the Christian has faith that He is.* That God is in full control. That *this* is the kind of world we live in.

Now, what difference should this belief make? If we really believe it, I mean.

Remember earlier where I tried to contrast "belief" and "faith" (p. 00)? To have faith, I said, thinking of the story of the lady and the tiger, means to open the door and go through. Real faith means staking our lives on what we believe.

Now, we never leave that kind of faith behind. That "stake your life on it" confidence is the most vital ingredient of your relationship with Christ. Because "you can *never* please God . . . without depending on him" (Heb. 11:6). And dependence is a fully active thing.

We sometimes have the opposite impression. We read a passage like this one: "What is faith? It is the confident assurance that something we want is going to happen. It is the certainty that what we hope for is waiting for us, even though we still cannot see it ahead of us" (Heb. 11:1). Sometimes we fasten on that word "wait" and read into it the idea that faith is sitting down! That if you wait long enough God will do something, and that He is delighted if you do nothing until He does something spectacular.

Just a moment's thought shows us this can't be true. How does a person act if he has the "certainty that what we hope for is waiting for us?" Well, suppose a girl has been waiting for days for a call from a certain special guy. Finally it comes; he asks her out for that Saturday night! Wow! What she's hoped for is finally going to happen.

So, what does she do Saturday? Sleep till noon, read till 4, talk on the phone till 5, eat and fool around till 6:30, and then settle down to watch TV? Never! She hops up and spends most of the day primping and fussing with her clothes and putting up her hair and all those other things girls do to fix themselves up. *When she really is sure that something she wants is going to happen, she acts like it!*

This is probably the hardest thing there is to learn in our new life with God. That we can, and must, put our lives on the line when He speaks to us, fully confident that God is going to work things out in the tangible world.

Remember the four kids in chapter 7 who described their Christian lives? One of their biggest hangups was about witnessing. How hard it seemed for them! Well, relying on God means that the next time we feel He is prompting us to speak about Christ, we're going to open our mouths and do it! Maybe we won't know what to say. Maybe we'll get laughed at. But relying on God means doing what He prompts us to do, and leaving the results completely up to Him. And we can do this freely, because He *does* intervene.

Now, this leaves us with some questions. So let's look at them.

How can we see God intervene? There are a number of different answers we could give to this one. We see Him in answered prayer. In changes in other people's attitude. In circumstances; things "working out." In discovering results of our choices we hadn't known about. And so on. But none of these answers is really satisfying.

What I mean is this. I could share experiences from my life to illustrate each of the thoughts above. But in each case it would be my belief that God had intervened that I'm talking about—not something *you* could see. Looking at these same incidents from outside, since in each case God worked within the framework of natural events, you might say, "You don't need God to explain *that!* It just happened."

The only way *you* can really see God intervene is to put your life on the line with Him. To actually begin to rely on Him. To act as He prompts you, and then let Him work out the results. The exciting thing is, then you'll know. Then you'll see for yourself. And His voice inside you will match up with the events, and suddenly you'll find yourself excited and thankful, because you'll know that God intervened for you. You saw Him.

What if things don't work out as we want? This one goes right back to the question of Who in the relationship is God. Acting and living by faith does not mean that we get what we want. It means that we let God take over and work what's *best*. And, what we want right now, and what's best, may be two different things! The Bible warns "Those who decide to please Jesus by living godly lives will suffer." (2 Tim. 3:12). So don't be surprised if some of your acts of faith work out "wrong."

But do remember this: God doesn't have the same view of hard times that we may have. We try to avoid them because we don't like them. He brings them into our lives because they're good for us. "Even though the going is rough for a while down here," the Bible says, "these trials are only to test your faith, that you may see whether or not it is strong and pure. It is being tested as fire tests gold and purifies it—and your faith is far more precious to God than mere gold" (1 Peter 1:6-7). And in another place Paul, who suffered many hardships, writes, "We can rejoice, too, when we run into problems and trials for we know they are good for us—they help us learn to be patient. And patience develops strength of character in us and helps us trust God more each time until finally our hope and faith are strong and steady. Then, when that happens, we will be able to hold our heads high no matter what happens and know that all is well, for we will know how dearly God loves us, and we will feel this warm love everywhere within us because God has given us the Holy Spirit to fill our hearts with his love" (Rom. 5:3-5).

So when things don't work out our way, we still trust and know things *are* working out God's way. We experience His love, and we still go on, putting our life on the line daily, because we believe that God is, and that He constantly intervenes in our world and guides our lives.

What if we don't feel God at all? This happens. "I think even the most mature Christian kid will ask, in times of depression or when things go hard, whether there really is a God." Our college friend here is right. The most mature Christian will have times when God seems far away; when things press hard and he's deeply depressed and when he wonders if there really is a God at all.

What then?

Christ was once tempted by the devil, the Bible tells us (Luke 4:1-12). Satan challenged Him to prove that God had not deserted Him. It was just after forty days of fasting in the wilderness, when He was weak and feeling down, that Satan suggested the Lord throw Himself off the pinnacle of the temple. "If You're really the Son of God," he said, "an angel will appear to catch You before You dash Your heel against a stone, because the Bible says God will do that for His Son." But Christ answered, "No. It is written, you shall not put the Lord your God to the test."

It's interesting to see where Christ got the "it is written" quote. It's from the Old Testament and it refers back to a time when God's people were in a wilderness too, without water and very thirsty. They had, over the past few months, seen God work in the physical world in many clear, miraculous interventions (Exod. 4-14). A supernatural cloud of fire had even led them to this particular part of the wilderness and, as they grumbled, was in plain sight overhead. And what did they demand to know? "Is God among us, or not?"

This is the kind of thing that puts all to the greatest challenge of all. The challenge of living by faith. Of committing ourselves, even if we can't see evidence that God is with us right now, to act on the assurance that He is, and that He will intervene for us.

So, what do we do if we can't feel God at all? We live by faith. We build our lives on God's Word. We refuse to demand that He show Himself to us—to "put God to the test." And when God's purposes in testing our faith are fulfilled, we see Him more clearly than ever before.

What is our part, then? Our part is what we've been thinking about throughout this chapter. Our part is to get to know God better—His way.

Too often we hear pat and simple answers on how to get to know Christ personally. Far too pat, and too mechanical. "Just read your Bible and pray," is probably one we hear most often. And this is important. But prayer and Bible study are important only within the context of, and as they focus on, the faith relationship we've described here. God really doesn't care if we whip through our ten verses of Scripture a day, dash off a seven-minute prayer, and go out to live our life as we want, stumbling after illusion upon illusion.

What does Christ want? What is our part in this relationship we have with God?

1. Get into the Word. Not as a duty, and certainly not to find rules you have to keep. But read the Bible to meet God, and to learn all you can about Him. And remember, it's in the Bible that you get the real scoop on what life is really all about.

2. Be responsible to what God says. Take Him

seriously when He applies His Word to your life, and do what He says. At first this kind of obedience may seem hard. But if you are responsive, and do obey, then "the way you live will always please the Lord and honor him," because you "will always be doing good, kind things for others, all the time learning to know God better and better" (Col. 1:10).

Remember, though, when you hear His command and you realize that you can't do it, that you don't have to. You simply turn to Christ who lives within you. You tell Him that you can't, and you take the step of faith and obey, trusting Him to do it for you. When you respond this way, "you will be filled up with his mighty, glorious strength so that you can keep on going no matter what happens—always full of the joy of the Lord (Col. 1:11).

3. Put your life on the line daily. Make decisions as if God really is in control of things and is ready to intervene for you. This really means *never worry about the consequences.* For "consequences" are the biggest mirage of all. Our part in a relationship with God isn't to figure out what will happen if we do this or do that. Our part is to do what Christ tells us, and expect Him to take care of the results.

This is terribly hard to learn. "If I do this, they'll laugh at me." "If I don't do this, they won't accept me." "If I act this way, I'll make a fool of myself." All these are natural fears that flood us when we face difficult decisions. But they're illusion. Illusions that make us lose our way and turn from complete obedience to God. What is the reality? That this *is* the kind of world where God is in control. So we have to respond to what He wants us to do, and not to our fears, if we want to find His way through life.

4. Don't ever expect to "arrive." This is something we haven't said right out, but it should be clear. The Christian life is a *growing relationship* with Christ.

So don't expect to experience all there is to relationship with God the first week. Or month. Or year. God will show you as much of Himself as you're ready to see. And when you're in that growing relationship, there's always more and better to come.

5. Finally, don't get too upset if you goof. You've had fallings out with your friends and family. And you'll probably have fallings out with God. There will be times when you don't want to do what He shows you. And when you won't do it.

At times like that you *could* turn to God and ask Him to help you want to obey. But sometimes you won't. I know I don't.

The great thing is, He's always ready when we're willing to come back. When we're ready to fit into the relationship His way—the only possible way because, after all, He is God.

And another great thing. No matter where you are in your relationship with Him right now, you can know that "God Who began the good work within you" when you first trusted Christ "will keep right on helping you grow in his grace until his task within you is finally finished on that day when Jesus Christ returns" (Phil. 1:6).

Steps to take

1. Someone once wrote, "If God seems far away, who do you think moved?" What's your reaction to this?

2. Where do you feel you are in your relationship

with God right now? What concepts in this chapter could help you understand why?

3. If you were to plan now to revamp your approach to relationships with God, what do you feel would be the most important steps you could take?

10

All together now!

"I had no knowledge of God," writes a New Jersey sophomore, "until I came in contact with those who really love Him. Through them I saw that He is the answer and that He lives and makes a difference in our lives."

She's pointing up something we often miss. That when it comes to growing in our relationship with God, others are important. In fact, growth really *has* to be something we do together.

Almost everyone of us is aware that others have an effect on us. But too often we're aware only of the *bad* effect. So many who shared in the preparation of this book wrote about hypocrisy. "Kids doubt Christianity," said one Pennsylvania seventeen-year-old, "because they see professing Christians, especially their parents, living for themselves and for the world as if their Christian experience meant nothing to them." A New York girl agrees. "Kids hate hypocrisy of any sort, and Christianity appears full of it. We rarely see anyone who practices Christianity in the true respect, who is also likeable."

Criticism isn't just leveled at adults. "We see Christian kids at school who live the same as non-Christians. If Christians act the same way they do, why be a Christian?"

This kind of thing dampens our enthusiasm when we decide we want to really follow Christ. Especially when sometimes we find that not only are we alone in our desire, but that other Christians seem to try to hurt and to block us. That can have disastrous effects! "Don, my nineteen-year-old cousin, turned playboy because he was forced to go to church," says a student at Philadelphia College of the Bible. "He was completely discouraged by the pious young people of the church. They tried to impress him with their spirituality but were so materialistic they made him feel too poor to attend church if he didn't have on the latest style of clothes. The 'elders' were severe with him because he attended dances and movies. They judged him as if they were without sins. The girl he had been dating, who also attended our 'House of Hypocrites,' was no better. He found out that she had been skipping school to hang around with boys in a nearby college. All in all, he is turned off on Christianity. From his point of view, I can't blame him."

Now, the thing to note here isn't how wrong others sometimes are. Or even that, really, this experience isn't a valid excuse for turning away from God. The thing to note is the power others do have in our lives for good or for evil; to help us or to hurt.

In the last few chapters we've been talking about growing in our relationship with Christ. Now we have to see that this kind of growth takes place best in the context of real Christian fellowship. When we help each other grow.

"When I doubted Christianity," says an Oregon fellow,

"it was, I now believe, because I had no older Christian who was a firm believer who would associate with me—integrate his ideas into me by friendly association. Then I met a vibrant Christian man of about thirty. We golfed and fished together—and he banished all doubt from my mind by his staunch belief and his support of it in his actions."

Because we can have this kind of impact on each other—an impact for which God has planned—the Bible encourages us to "talk with each other much about the Lord" (Eph. 5:19). And because God planned this context of warm personal friendships with other Christians, the Bible uses one little phrase over and over again.

What is it?

"Each other"

The Bible uses an analogy when it talks about the relationship of Christians to each other. It's the picture of the body. Each of us who are in relationship with Christ are viewed as part of this body, and thus as being in the closest kind of relationship with each other.

In talking about this, the Bible always emphasizes the way we parts of the body are to care for each other. "Have the same care for each other," it says, that you do for yourselves. "If one part suffers, all the parts suffer with it, and if one part is honored, all the parts are glad. Now here is what I am trying to say: all of you together are the one body of Christ and each one of you is a separate and necessary part of it" (1 Cor. 12:25-27).

How are we *necessary?* In another place we're told that "each part [each one of us] in its own special way helps the other parts, so that the whole body is healthy and growing and full of love" (Eph. 4:16). For each of us to grow in the Lord, all of us need to grow together. And in growing together we each have something to share with others.

Sometimes we can warn another person when he gets off track. "Beware then of your own hearts, dear brothers, lest you find that they, too, are evil and unbelieving and are leading you away from the living God. Speak to each other about these things every day while there is still time, so that none of you will become hardened against God, being blinded by the glamour of sin" (Heb. 3:12-13). Don could have used this kind of help from someone who cared, instead of the cold criticism he received.

Sometimes helping is just listening to and caring about someone. "Make me truly happy," the Bible asks, "by loving each other and agreeing wholeheartedly with each other, working together with one heart and mind and purpose. Don't be selfish; don't live to make a good impression on others. Be humble, thinking of others as better than yourself. Don't think just about your own affairs, but be interested in others, too, and in what they are doing" (Phil. 2:2-4).

"When I became a freshman in high school I became a member of the Teens group at church," wrote Carolyn. "I was really excited about this until I found out that I was the only one my age; the only freshman in the group of forty teens. I didn't fit into any of the cliques. Nobody paid attention to me, except for an occasional 'Hi. How are you?' Everyone was concerned with his own status and identification."

How did this affect her? "When I thought of going to a youth meeting I had mixed emotions. I felt very rejected, yet desperately wanted to be one of the group. So instead of sitting home I went to the meetings, wondering if I would ever really become one of them."

This hurt Carolyn, surely. But it actually hurt the rest of the group too! How? "Dear friends," the Apostle John wrote, "since God loved us as much as that [sending his Son to die for us], we surely ought to love each other too. For though we have never yet seen God, when we love each other God lives in us and his love within us grows ever stronger" (1 John 4:11-12). See it? *It's by loving others and sharing ourselves with them that God's life and love grow within us.*

What happens when we turn inward, reject others, and refuse to become involved in their lives? "Whoever loves his fellow man is 'walking in the light' and can see his way without stumbling around in darkness and sin. But he who dislikes [rejecting another person or refusing to care about him is just that!] his brother is wandering around in spiritual darkness, and doesn't know where he is going, for the darkness has made him blind so that he cannot see the way" (1 John 2:10-11).

Our own growth depends on our loving others too!

Finally, and most important, we help each other by sharing our experiences of Christ. "Remember what Christ taught and let his words enrich your lives and make you wise; teach them to each other and sing them out in psalms and hymns and spiritual songs, singing to the Lord with thankful hearts" (Col. 3:16). This is helping too—perhaps the biggest help we can possibly give, or get. For we experience Christ to the fullest when our experience is shared with others.

All this has many practical implications for us. What are some of them?

If you're on the inside, think of others. Don't pick your friends for the status they give you. After a time Carolyn did become a part of the group. "In my remaining years in Teens I've become a leader and officer in the group, but I'm very thankful for the experience of rejection I went through my freshman year. It helps me to empathize with those who never become very popular. I know how they can feel left out, and therefore can better understand and help them."

This fits exactly with what God wants to do in your life: to love others through you. "Most of all," the Bible says, "let love guide your life" (Col. 3:14). As a sixteen-year-old wrote me, "Treat Christians as you would Christ—remember He is in them. This will be revolutionizing. It's by our love for one another that all men know we're His disciples."

If you're on the outside, think of others. Sometimes when we're on the outside, because it does hurt, we begin to think only of ourselves. We feel sorry for ourselves, and resent others. What are we to do if we've been rejected? We reach out—we love.

Even when we're hurt and rebuffed? Yes, even then. "Be gentle and ready to forgive; never hold grudges. Remember, the Lord forgave you, so you must forgive others" (Col. 3:13).

The time will come, as it did for Carolyn, when you're accepted. And then you'll be better for your sufferings, because you'll understand how others can be hurt as you've been. And you'll love them better.

Share Christ's life with others. Maybe at first you won't have a group of other Christians who want to go on with the Lord. But do search out one or two. And get together with them to share.

Sharing is the key to going on with Christ together. It means talking openly together about how you really feel—even when you're down or have doubts. It means telling each other what Christ is doing in your lives. Talking about how His word has reached you. Telling how He's helping you become a new person inside, and helping you by intervening in the tangible world. And it means caring about each other, listening to each other, praying for each other, giving yourself for the others even when it costs you something. And it is vital for a growing, healthy life with Christ.

So try it. And see how much more quickly Christ comes into focus, and you discover that He is very, very real—to you.

Very, very real

In chapter 1 you accepted an invitation to doubt. An

invitation to ask the questions Is God real? and Is God necessary—to me?

In a way, we end our exploration into doubt with no answer. We really haven't proven God. Not in the scientific, test-tube way so many people want. We haven't measured or weighed Him, or made Him run through a maze, as the psychologists do a rat, to see how He'll perform. We haven't attached electrodes to His skull, to read His brain waves. So if you were looking for this kind of answer, you're bound to be disappointed. This kind of answer just can't be given. God doesn't perform for us, on our call.

What have we seen? We've seen some traces of God's work in human personality. We've seen the emptiness that underlies all life apart from God—an emptiness you may have experienced. And we've seen the morality gap, that chasm between what we think we ought to do and what we actually do. All of us have experienced that.

So we have made some progress. In a way. I hope that we've made enough progress so that whoever reads this book, and especially you, has at least clarified the issues.

Because the issue in a question like this one is never one of evidence. It's always one of faith.

As we saw, everyone—even the most scientific of us —ultimately takes his stand by faith. The way he lives, the choices he makes, the values he chooses, all reflect the kind of world he believes this world really is. And this view always rests on faith—faith that God is, or faith that God is not.

We've said some things about faith too. Particularly to show that it's different from belief. You may *say* you believe in God, but what you *do* shows where your faith actually rests! It's the same with all of us. And I suspect that many people who are criticized for being hypocrites aren't that at all. They're just people who think that they believe, but who don't have faith at all.

It's possible—even probable—that all of us have been in that boat. You too.

That's why I said at the beginning of this book that I think doubt is a good thing. In fact, I think it's great! Because when we doubt we're forced to take an honest look at where we are. We ask whether God is, surely. But we also look at ourselves. At our own faith. What kind of faith is it? Is it just ideas we've picked up from church, or from mom and dad? Or is our faith the kind of dependence on God that the Bible talks about—that hanging ourselves out on a limb and acting on what God says to us, because we believe that He really is, and because we're confident that He is really working in our lives?

That first kind of belief—the saying of holy words—is the stuff hypocrisy is made of. The second kind—putting our life where we say our trust is—is what reality is made of. This is the thing we come up against when we doubt: we must look at ourselves, and we have to decide for ourselves.

The decision is always made before we have the proof. No one experiences God until he decides to rely fully on Him and to come to Him His way. And this way is simple—but hard.

That's why we had to spend those chapters on describing what the Bible says is the way to know God. Not to "know about" God, but to know *Him.* To experience Him.

And that's where we have to end. With that invitation. Not the invitation to doubt—but the invitation to find out.

So, why not accept this invitation too?

Go ahead.

Dig in and find out—for yourself.

Steps to take

1. If a person decides *not* to accept the invitation to find out for himself, would it be honest for him to say later, "I don't know if God exists"? What do you think?

2. The author suggests that when we finish the book, we stand on the brink of decision. What kind of decision would be called for from a person who—
   a. has never become a Christian?
   b. is unsure if he is a Christian, or if he has been operating all this time on "belief"?
   c. is a Christian, but is very uncertain about his relationship with God?
   d. has experienced the reality of God, but wants to know more?
   e. is like you?

3. If you still have questions (and you may well have them) just jot them down, and go back over the book looking for answers. Or talk them over with friends. But remember, it always comes back to one issue—you decide.

4. What kind of a decision are you going to make?

Notes

Chapter 1

[1]Over 3,000 high schoolers and college students contributed their thoughts as this book was being written. Every quote is authentic, saying what fellows and girls really think and feel. You may not agree with all of them, and I may not agree, but we want them to tell it like it is.

Chapter 2

[1]Alvin N. Rogness, *Youth Asks, Why Bother About God?* (New York: Nelson, 1965), p. 9.

[2]"Dope in the Suburbs: Teens Tell It Like It Is," *Chicago Daily News* (December 16, 1968), p. 1.

[3]C. S. Lewis, *Mere Christianity* (New York: Macmillan, 1967), p. 2.

[4]*Ibid.*

Chapter 3

[1]Graham T. Blaine, *Youth and the Hazards of Affluence* (New York: Harper & Row, 1966), pp. 118-19.

[2]Jacques Barzun, *The American University* (New York: Harper & Row, 1968), pp. 79-80.

[3]David E. Kucharsky, "A Case for the Young," *Christianity Today* (October 11, 1968), p. 3.

[4]J. B. Phillips, *Plain Christianity* (London: Epworth, 1960), p. 79.

Chapter 5

[1]Arthur F. Holmes, *Christianity and Philosophy* (Chicago: Inter-Varsity, 1960), p. 16.

[2]H. M. Morris and J. C. Whitcomb, *The Genesis Flood* (Grand Rapids: Baker, 1961), pp. 443, 450.

[3]D. Dwight David, cited in Morris and Whitcomb, p. 450.

[4]I'm aware that you may want a lot more information on this question of science and Scripture than I give in this book. If you are troubled about the conflict of viewpoints or, like the girl quoted earlier, find yourself on the defensive and want some specific answers, let me suggest a few resources.

For a general coverage of the question of evolution, check Paul A. Zimmerman (ed.), *Darwin, Evolution, and Creation* (St. Louis: Concordia, 1959). For a specific and careful study of biological evolution, and reasoned objections to the evolutionists' big picture, read John W. Klotz, *Genes, Genesis, and Evolution* (St. Louis: Concordia, 1955). When questions of the Genesis flood come up, see Henry M. Morris and John C. Whitcomb, Jr.'s work, *The Genesis Flood* (Grand Rapids, Baker, 1961). A good overview of intellectual questions is contained in Paul E. Little's *Know Why You Believe* (Wheaton, Ill.: Scripture Press, 1967). And for some interesting and compelling arguments as to why the weight of evidence rests with the Bible, Peter Stoner's little book *Science Speaks* (Chicago: Moody, 1958) is excellent.

After reading these you can decide for yourself where the weight of evidence lies.

[5]For an interesting presentation of this see C. S. Lewis' little book *The Problem of Pain* (New York: Macmillan, 1946). All of the books mentioned in this chapter can probably be found at your Christian bookstore.

Chapter 6

[1]If you're troubled about either of these ideas, why not take a look at such books as W. Graham Scroggie, *Is the Bible the Word of God?* (Chicago: Moody, 1922), and Bernard Ramm's *Protestant Christian Evidences* (Chicago: Moody, 1953).

[2]Lewis, p. 122.

Chapter 7

[1]Rogness, p. 76.

Chapter 9

[1]Just how to know this kind of leading, and how to make hard decisions by relying on God, are discussed in chapters 9 and 10 of an earlier book in this series, *How I Can Be Real* (Zondervan, 1979).